WORKBOOK

THE
GOSPEL WAY
CATECHISM

TREVIN WAX
AND THOMAS WEST

HARVEST HOUSE PUBLISHERS
EUGENE, OREGON

Published in association with the literary agency of Wolgemuth & Wilson.

Cover design and illustration by Faceout Studio, Spencer Fuller
Interior illustrations by Spencer Fuller
Interior design by Janelle Coury

For bulk, special sales, or ministry purchases, please call 1-800-547-8979.
Email: CustomerService@hhpbooks.com

The Gospel Way Catechism Workbook

Copyright © 2025 by Trevin Wax and Thomas West
Published by Harvest House Publishers
Eugene, Oregon 97408
www.HarvestHousePublishers.com

ISBN 978-0-7369-9143-8 (pbk)
ISBN 978-0-7369-9144-5 (eBook)

CONTENTS

INTRODUCTION
Why Counter-Catechism?

WELCOME TO *THE GOSPEL WAY Catechism Workbook*! This resource is designed to give you more than just a summary of truths or a set of fill-in-the-blank exercises. It's meant to help you take the truths in the primary resource, *The Gospel Way Catechism*, and dig deeper, reflect more fully, and take the ancient, countercultural truths of Christianity and incorporate them in your everyday life.

Unlike the main catechism, which introduces you to the enduring truths of the faith, this workbook invites you into a more personal journey. Here you have space to wrestle with additional questions, think carefully, and respond thoughtfully. We hope these questions will spark reflection, challenge assumptions, and help you see how the Scriptures help you rethink and resist the prevalent cultural narratives of our time.

We live in a world that pulls us in a thousand directions. Moments of stillness—moments to reflect deeply on the things that matter most—are rare these days. This workbook is geared toward contemplation. It's more than a tool for study, or a checklist to rush through during the week. It's an invitation to slow down, to step back, and to consider more deeply how the story of Scripture shapes how we see ourselves, our world, and our Savior.

The goal of this resource is simple: to help you see Christianity not as a distant set of doctrines to observe, but as the lens through which to make sense of everything. Whether you're a longtime believer in need of a fresh reminder of how distinct and glorious the Christian faith is, or a new Christian learning how to think biblically in a changing world, this workbook is designed to lead you to deeper thought, greater clarity, and renewed joy in the gospel way of Jesus Christ.

How to Use This Workbook

WORKING YOUR WAY THROUGH A catechism is a process designed for slowness and contemplation, not speed and superficiality. Here are a few suggestions on how to make the most of this workbook.

- **Memorize:** Catechism questions and answers are designed to be memorized. There is a rhythm and art to the wording, intended to aid the memory. We recommend spending five to ten minutes every day for a full week with each question, carefully considering the answer, and committing it to memory so you can recite it word for word.

- **Summary:** The summary for each question explains the concept in a little more detail, showing how Christianity stands in contrast to what often passes for common sense in the world today.

- **Reflection Questions:** The bold text is drawn from the book, *The Gospel Way Catechism*, but specific answers to the questions that follow aren't found in the book. Reflection questions give you an opportunity to look at your life in light of Christian teaching and then look for ways to apply the truth to your life. We recommend journaling through the reflection questions throughout the week, before moving on to the next question and answer. Pray through this part of the process.

- **Scriptures to Ponder:** The Bible verses we've included in this workbook will help you see how God's Word is the basis for the Christian truths expounded in the catechism. We've left space for you to journal your thoughts on these important passages of Scripture.

- **Prayer from Church History:** We are not the first Christians to encounter these foundational truths. We stand in a long line of faithfulness, bearing witness to the fruit of a tree planted two thousand years ago, with roots that go down deep. These prayers from church history are designed to help you align your voice and your heart with faithful men and women who have gone before us.

- **Find a partner or group:** One of the best ways to work through a catechism is with brothers and sisters in your church. We recommend enlisting a partner to walk through the process at the same time, for accountability and inspiration, or joining a church group that commits to this process for 50 weeks. Discussing the Christian faith with others will solidify these truths in ways that going solo will not.

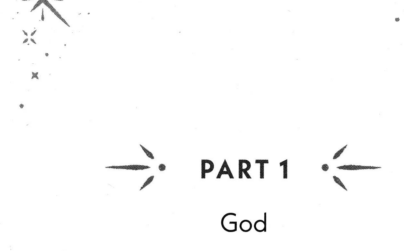

PART 1

God

QUESTION 1

What Is the Center and Point of Everything?

ANSWER

God is the center and point of everything. In him, all things
come to be and are held together. He has no rival.

SUMMARY

The gospel way challenges the contemporary notion that we are the masters of our fate and the captains of our souls. In modern Western culture, the constant emphasis on self-determination and individualism often leads to loneliness and exhaustion. The Bible changes the picture. Instead of seeking meaning within ourselves, we find true purpose and fulfillment in God. The Bible begins with God, emphasizing that our lives should revolve around him. When we place God at the center, we receive our identity and purpose from him, leading to a stable and fulfilling life. God, not us, is the center. His glory is the point of everything that exists.

REFLECTION QUESTIONS

Content in bold comes from *The Gospel Way Catechism*, pages 14-15.

1. **The world tells us, "My ultimate purposes are those which arise within me; the crucial meanings of things are those defined in my responses to them."**[1] In a culture that promotes self-determined purpose, how does recognizing God as the ultimate source of meaning and purpose reshape your understanding of your own life's significance? Reflect on how this shift in perspective can impact the way you make decisions and prioritize your goals.

2. **The world tells us, "You come first."** Why does this seem at first like good news? Why would the Bible tell us it's bad news? How does the truth that meaning and purpose come from God shape your understanding of your identity and purpose?

3. **We suffer under the weight and pressure of constantly having to figure out who we are, what our future should be, and what will make us happy. Jesus tells us,** *Seek God first* **(Matthew 6:33).** What risks and pressures are associated with having to figure out who we are, what our future looks like, and what determines our happiness?

4. **The world doesn't revolve around us, and neither does God. It is** *we* **who revolve around** *him*. How does the realization that we revolve around God, rather than him revolving around us, change your perspective on your daily decisions and priorities? How can understanding that God is the center around which we revolve help you build a more God-centered approach to worship and prayer?

5. **The Bible begins with these words: "In the beginning God…" (Genesis 1:1).** Why is it important that the Bible begins with God as the first character to appear? How does starting with God as the center influence the way you live your daily life?

SCRIPTURES TO PONDER

What do these Scripture passages tell us about God's action in creating the world, and his ultimate purpose?

- **Genesis 1:1:** "In the beginning God created the heavens and the earth."

- **Colossians 1:16-17:** "Everything was created by him, in heaven and on earth, the visible and the invisible, whether thrones or dominions or rulers or authorities—all things have been created through him and for him. He is before all things, and by him all things hold together."

- **Matthew 6:33:** "Seek first the kingdom of God and his righteousness, and all these things will be provided for you."

PRAYER FROM CHURCH HISTORY

You, oh Lord, are great and worthy of exceeding praise. Your great virtue and your wisdom are beyond comprehension. Humanity, though merely creatures, longs to praise you—the same humanity that bears the weight of mortality, the testimony of sin, and the reminder that you resist the proud. Still, humanity, this small part of your creation, inherently desires to praise you. You enkindle in us a longing to praise you because you have made us for yourself, and our hearts are restless until they rest in you.

—Augustine of Hippo (354–430)[2]

QUESTION 2
How Do We See God and Come to Know Him?

ANSWER

We see God by the light of his revelation, not by our imagination. God reveals his character and purposes through his Word and works.

SUMMARY

The gospel way focuses on the importance of divine revelation over personal imagination in understanding God. Modern secular thought often posits that individuals create their own meaning and reality. This perspective is epitomized by Protagoras's statement, "Man is the measure of all things."[1] In contrast, the Bible asserts that true understanding comes from God's revelation. There are two types of revelation: general (through creation) and special (through Scripture). While creation reveals something of God's character, it is through the Bible that we see God most clearly. Scripture acts as a lens, helping us interpret reality and understand God's nature and purposes.

REFLECTION QUESTIONS

Content in bold comes from *The Gospel Way Catechism*, pages 17-18.

1. **We set the standard. We determine morality.** How does this statement contrast with the biblical perspective that God's revelation is the ultimate standard for adjudicating truth? How do these contrasting perspectives shape one's understanding of reality and morality?

2. **We can either seek to interpret the world through the story told in the Scriptures or through the story of self.** Do you struggle to keep these two stories separated in your own thinking and living? In what ways do you practically experience these stories competing for your attention and affection?

3. **Creation bears his fingerprints. General revelation is wonderful, but it only takes us so far.** What are some attributes of God that are made plain to you as you observe God's creation? What can we learn about God's character and works?

4. **Special revelation refers to God's Word (the Bible). We see God most clearly in how he reveals himself through his Word.** What are some of the attributes of God that are made clear to us in Scripture? In what ways has the Bible provided you with a clearer understanding of God's character and his purpose for your life?

5. **In the end, we know God because God has made himself known. We do not conjure up God as we'd like to imagine; we encounter God as he has revealed himself.** How does regular engagement with Scripture—the enduring Word of God that remains forever—shape how you interpret events, make choices, and interact with others?

SCRIPTURES TO PONDER

What do we learn about God from these Scriptures about creation?

- **Psalm 19:1-2:** "The heavens declare the glory of God, and the expanse proclaims the work of his hands. Day after day they pour out speech; night after night they communicate knowledge."

- **Romans 1:20:** "His invisible attributes, that is, his eternal power and divine nature, have been clearly seen since the creation of the world, being understood through what he has made. As a result, people are without excuse."

What does this passage about the Scriptures teach us about God's purpose in revealing himself?

- **2 Timothy 3:16-17:** "All Scripture is inspired by God and is profitable for teaching, for rebuking, for correcting, for training in righteousness, so that the man of God may be complete, equipped for every good work."

PRAYER FROM CHURCH HISTORY

O my God, teach my heart where and how to seek you, where and how to find you. You are my God and you are my all and I have never seen you. You have made me and remade me, you have showered upon me all the good things I possess, still I do not know you. I have not yet done that for which I was made. Teach me to seek you. I cannot seek you unless you teach me or find you unless you show yourself to me. Let me seek you in my desire, let me desire you in my seeking. Let me find you by loving you, let me love you when I find you.

—Anselm of Canterbury (1033–1109)[2]

QUESTION 3
Who Does God Reveal Himself to Be?

ANSWER

He is the Lord, the great I AM, one God in three persons: Father, Son, and Spirit. He is the Creator and Ruler of all that is, seen and unseen.

SUMMARY

The gospel way contrasts sharply with the nihilistic vision of Friedrich Nietzsche, who saw life as meaningless and God as a great deception. In contrast, Christianity reveals a purposeful life rooted in the existence of God, who is not just the greatest being but Being itself. God is personal, relational, the Creator and Sustainer of all things, and reveals himself in Scripture as the Great I AM. This name, revealed to Moses, signifies God's eternal presence, self-sufficiency, and sovereign power. The Bible further reveals God as the Trinity—Father, Son, and Spirit—providing a relational framework for understanding purpose, meaning, and community. This triune God is the source of transcendence and a fountain of self-giving love.

REFLECTION QUESTIONS

Content in bold comes from *The Gospel Way Catechism*, pages 20-21.

1. **In a world that often lives as if there is no God, or as if God is whatever we imagine him to be, or as if God is just one of many potential deities, Christianity, like a comet streaking across the sky, declares the identity of the God who made us.** What are some differences between these ways of living: (1) as if there is no God, (2) as if God is whatever we want him to be, (3) as if God is just one of many gods, or (4) according to the Bible's presentation of who God is?

2. The first sentence of the Bible says, "In the beginning God created the heavens and the earth" (Genesis 1:1). What are the implications of viewing God as the source of all creation rather than seeing the universe as a product of random chance? How does the belief that God is the Creator affect your perspective on your relationship with the world and others? How does accepting God as the Creator challenge the pressure to define yourself by societal standards or personal achievements?

3. **God revealed his name to Moses in Exodus 3:14: "I AM WHO I AM."** How does understanding God as unchanging and eternal influence the way you approach life's uncertainties and challenges? In what ways do God's attributes of wisdom and power provide comfort and guidance in times of decision-making? How do God's unchanging nature and truth impact your trust in his promises, even when circumstances seem uncertain?

4. **As you move through the Bible, the revelation of God grows brighter and clearer. The one true God, the Great I AM, is the Father, the Son, and the Spirit.** How does the relational nature of the Trinity offer a framework for understanding purpose, meaning, and community?

5. **Christianity claims the majestic, awe-inspiring, holy God of love exists as Father, Son, and Spirit, that self-giving love is the key to the mystery of life, and that all the goodness and happiness in the world can be traced back to the fountain of all joy, the divine dance of God at the center of all things.** How does believing God as the ultimate authority and sustainer of all things shape your understanding of reality and influence your daily decisions, values, and sense of security?

SCRIPTURES TO PONDER

What do these Scriptures show us about who God is and what our response to his revelation should be?

- **Exodus 3:14:** "God replied to Moses, 'I AM WHO I AM. This is what you are to say to the Israelites: I AM has sent me to you.'"

- **Isaiah 43:10:** "'You are my witnesses'—this is the Lord's declaration—'and my servant whom I have chosen, so that you may know and believe me and understand that I am he. No god was formed before me, and there will be none after me.'"

- **John 1:1-3:** "In the beginning was the Word, and the Word was with God, and the Word was God. He was with God in the beginning. All things were created through him, and apart from him not one thing was created that has been created."

PRAYER FROM CHURCH HISTORY

Almighty and everlasting God, you have given to us your servants grace, by the confession of a true faith, to acknowledge the glory of the eternal Trinity, and in the power of your divine Majesty to worship the Unity: Keep us steadfast in this faith and worship, and bring us at last to see you in your one and eternal glory, O Father; who with the Son and the Holy Spirit live and reign, one God, for ever and ever. Amen.

—*The Book of Common Prayer*[1]

Who Is God the Father?

ANSWER

God the Father is the Almighty One, infinitely great and good, whose name is hallowed in heaven and on earth. He is not a distant authority, but a holy God filled with fatherly love.

SUMMARY

The gospel way teaches us to see God the Father not through the lens of our earthly experiences but through the revelation of Scripture. While many may struggle with the idea of God as Father due to negative paternal experiences, the Bible consistently portrays God as the perfect Father—infinitely great, good, and filled with fatherly love. He is life-giving, majestic, and compassionate, providing wisdom, comfort, and discipline. This understanding of God reshapes our view of authority and power, showing us a God who delights in loving and guiding us, inviting us to trust in his plans and draw close to him.

REFLECTION QUESTIONS

Content in bold comes from *The Gospel Way Catechism*, pages 24-25.

1. **The Apostles' Creed begins this way: "I believe in God the Father Almighty, creator of heaven and earth."** What is the significance of recognizing God as both loving Father and almighty Creator? What goes wrong if only one aspect is emphasized, to the exclusion of the other?

2. **He is not a distant authority, but a holy God filled with fatherly love.** Reflect on how this understanding of God influences your relationship with him. How does seeing God as both authoritative and loving change your perspective on obedience and trust?

3. **God the Father is the Almighty One, infinitely great and good.** In what ways does recognizing God's greatness and goodness affect your daily life and decisions? How does this shape your understanding of God's plans for you?

4. **The Bible consistently portrays God as the perfect Father—infinitely great, good, and filled with fatherly love.** What are some ways that earthly fathers give us a glimpse of our heavenly Father? What are some ways that earthly fathers always fall short of God's infinite goodness?

5. **He is life-giving, majestic, and compassionate, providing wisdom, comfort, and discipline.** Reflect on these attributes of God and why it's important that they go together and are not separated or isolated from a comprehensive portrait of who God the Father reveals himself to be.

SCRIPTURES TO PONDER

What do these Scriptures teach us about relating to God as our Father?

- **Deuteronomy 32:6:** "Is this how you repay the LORD, you foolish and senseless people? Isn't he your Father and Creator? Didn't he make you and sustain you?"

- **Psalm 103:13:** "As a father has compassion on his children, so the LORD has compassion on those who fear him."

- **Matthew 6:9:** "You should pray like this: Our Father in heaven, your name be honored as holy."

PRAYER FROM CHURCH HISTORY

In your mercy, place in our hearts a comfortable confidence in your fatherly love. Make us taste and feel the sweetness of childlike trust, so that we may with joy call you Father. So that we may know and love you. So that we may call upon you for everything we need… You are not like an earthly father who cannot help himself. You have shown us how immeasurably better a Father you are. So grant us, Father, that we may also be your heavenly children.

—MARTIN LUTHER (1483–1546)[1]

QUESTION 5

Who Is God the Son?

ANSWER

God the Son is the eternal Word who took on humanity: Jesus of Nazareth, the Messiah of Israel and King of the world. He is not a life coach or therapist who affirms all our desires, but the Great Physician whose blood heals our sin-sick hearts.

SUMMARY

The gospel way teaches us that God the Son is not a manufactured version of a life coach or therapist who merely affirms our desires. Jesus of Nazareth, as revealed in the Gospels, is the eternal Word, the Messiah of Israel, and the King of the world. He took on humanity, fulfilling ancient prophecies and claiming his role as the climax of Israel's story. Jesus is the Great Physician, offering healing for our deepest needs through his self-sacrifice. Unlike cultural or personal versions of Jesus that align with our preferences, the true Jesus challenges us, offering a new direction and a profound transformation of our hearts.

REFLECTION QUESTIONS

Content in bold comes from *The Gospel Way Catechism*, pages 27-28.

1. **The world is full of manufactured ideas about Jesus. You can find just about any version of Jesus that suits you.** What are some of the most common versions of Jesus we see in society today?

2. **God the Son is the eternal Word who took on humanity: Jesus of Nazareth, the Messiah of Israel and King of the world.** How does this definition differ from worldly, manufactured ideas about Jesus?

3. **In the end, we don't need a coach; we need a Savior. We don't need an anesthetic; we need a surgeon. We don't need a heart tune-up; we need a heart transplant.** Our need for Jesus is far greater than we can understand because the depths of our sin are deeper than we imagine. Why is it so easy for people today to settle for a lesser Jesus than what we see in the Gospels?

4. **Unlike cultural or personal versions of Jesus that align with our preferences, the true Jesus challenges us, offering a new direction and a profound transformation of our hearts.** How can recognizing Jesus as the Messiah of Israel in fulfillment of God's ancient plan help you learn to trust in his promises?

5. **Jesus of Nazareth, as revealed in the Gospels, is the eternal Word, the Messiah of Israel, and the King of the world.** How does understanding Jesus as King of the world influence your daily decisions, values, and sense of security?

SCRIPTURES TO PONDER

What do these Scriptures teach us about the Son of God and what he reveals about God's character and power?

- **John 1:1-3:** "In the beginning was the Word, and the Word was with God, and the Word was God. He was with God in the beginning. All things were created through him, and apart from him not one thing was created that has been created."

- **Colossians 1:15-17:** "He is the image of the invisible God, the firstborn over all creation. For everything was created by him, in heaven and on earth, the visible and the invisible, whether thrones or dominions or rulers or authorities—all things have been created through him and for him. He is before all things, and by him all things hold together."

- **Hebrews 1:1-3:** "Long ago God spoke to our ancestors by the prophets at different times and in different ways. In these last days, he has spoken to us by his Son. God has appointed him heir of all things and made the universe through him. The Son is the radiance of God's glory and the exact expression of his nature, sustaining all things by his powerful word. After making purification for sins, he sat down at the right hand of the Majesty on high."

PRAYER FROM CHURCH HISTORY

Grant, most sweet and loving Jesus, that I may seek my repose in you above every creature; above all health and beauty; above every honor and glory; every power and dignity; above all knowledge and cleverness, all riches and arts, all joy and gladness; above all fame and praise, all sweetness and consolation; above every hope and promise, every merit and desire; above all the gifts and favors that you can give or pour down on me; above all the joy and exultation that the mind can receive and feel; and finally, above the angels and archangels and all the heavenly host; above all things visible and invisible; and may I seek my repose in you above everything that is not you, my God. For you, O Lord my God, are above all things the best. You alone are most high, you alone most powerful. You alone are most sufficient and most satisfying. You alone most sweet and consoling. You alone are most beautiful and loving, you alone most noble and glorious above all things. In you is every perfection that has been or ever will be. Therefore, whatever you give me besides yourself, whatever you reveal to me concerning yourself, and whatever you promise, is too small and insufficient when I do not see and fully enjoy you alone. For my heart cannot rest or be fully content until, rising above all gifts and every created thing, it rests in you.

—Thomas a Kempis (1380–1471)[1]

QUESTION 6
Who Is God the Spirit?

ANSWER

God the Spirit is the empowering presence of God in the world—the Lord, the giver of life. We are defined not by our inner self or spirituality, but by the Spirit's presence as he makes us new and blesses the world through our service in Jesus's name.

SUMMARY

The gospel way challenges the contemporary notion of spirituality as a personalized quest for transcendence, often expressed through self-focused practices like mindfulness and wellness rituals. True fulfillment is found not in these individualistic pursuits but in the Holy Spirit, who is presented in the Bible as God's personal and active presence in believers' lives. The Holy Spirit guides, convicts, empowers, and aligns believers with God's purpose. The Nicene Creed describes the Spirit as "the Lord, the giver of life," highlighting his role in creation and renewal. True life change and service to others come through the Spirit's power, embodying the glory of the Trinity.

REFLECTION QUESTIONS

Content in bold comes from *The Gospel Way Catechism*, pages 31-32.

1. **The Nicene Creed (AD 381), which lays out a clear description of the Trinity—one God in three persons—describes the Holy Spirit as "the Lord, the giver of life."** Why is it important to see the Holy Spirit as "the Lord"—equal with God the Father and God the Son, and what does his identity as the "giver of life" mean for you for as a believer?

2. **The Spirit is available not to bring about personal enlightenment or to give us a "spiritual side," but to align our lives with God's purpose and standard.** Describe the dangers of looking to God for a dash of "spirituality" in your life rather than relying on the Spirit to align your life with God's plan.

3. **It's common for people to think of the Spirit as a kind of energy or force, but the Scriptures describe the Spirit in personal terms.** What do we miss when we think of the Spirit and his work in impersonal ways? Why does it matter that the Spirit is a person, not merely a force?

4. **In a world where people are attracted to all kinds of spiritual practices, the Bible reminds us of the importance of the Spirit in bringing about real and lasting life change.** What are some ways we attempt to bring about life change apart from the power of the Spirit? Why are these attempts so often temporary instead of long-lasting?

5. **This is the glory of the Trinity, the central tenet of the Christian faith: the Father, the Son, and the Spirit are one God, the same in substance, equal in power and glory.** What are some aspects of this teaching about God as Father, Son, and Holy Spirit that you find difficult to understand? Why is this doctrine about God so important?

SCRIPTURES TO PONDER

What do these Scriptures teach us about God the Spirit and his work in our lives?

- **John 16:13:** "When the Spirit of truth comes, he will guide you into all the truth. For he will not speak on his own, but he will speak whatever he hears. He will also declare to you what is to come."

- **Ephesians 1:13-14:** "In him you also were sealed with the promised Holy Spirit when you heard the word of truth, the gospel of your salvation, and when you believed. The Holy Spirit is the down payment of our inheritance, until the redemption of the possession, to the praise of his glory."

- **Romans 8:26-27:** "In the same way the Spirit also helps us in our weakness, because we do not know what to pray for as we should, but the Spirit himself intercedes for us with inexpressible groanings. And he who searches our hearts knows the mind of the Spirit, because he intercedes for the saints according to the will of God."

PRAYER FROM CHURCH HISTORY

Holy Spirit, our hearts are naturally polluted: come into them, we pray, and work sin out, and work grace in. Make our hearts temples of purity and a paradise for pleasantness. Sanctify our imaginations, causing them to mint holy meditations. Sanctify our wills, biasing them to good, so it will be as delightful for us to serve God as once it was to sin against him. Perfume us with holiness and make our hearts a map of heaven.

—Thomas Watson (1620–1686)[1]

PART 2

Creation and Identity

QUESTION 7
Why Did God Create the World?

ANSWER
God created everything by his Word, not because he was lonely, but out of the free overflow of divine love, so that all creation would enjoy his glory.

SUMMARY

In contrast to common understandings of God as Creator, the Scriptures describe God creating the world not out of loneliness or necessity but from the overflow of his divine love, intending that all creation would enjoy his glory. This foundational Christian belief stands in contrast to naturalistic views that attribute the universe's existence to mere natural causes. Unlike the notion that humans must create their own meaning in a purposeless world, the Bible teaches that God, in his eternal happiness as Father, Son, and Spirit, created everything through the power of his Word. Our purpose and meaning are discovered in aligning with God's design, as creation is the theater of his glory.

REFLECTION QUESTIONS

Content in bold comes from *The Gospel Way Catechism*, pages 36-37.

1. **God created everything by his Word, not because he was lonely, but out of the free overflow of divine love.** Sometimes we project our own experiences and understandings onto God. We know what it feels like to be lonely and need a friend. God never experiences that. God—Father, Son, and Spirit—has always existed in a fellowship of perfect love. By creating us, God invites us into this fellowship of love. How does this reframe your understanding of community? How does the goal of love come into focus for you when you think of God's creative act in this way?

2. How does acknowledging that all creation brings glory to God compare with Carl Sagan's perspective that "the cosmos is within us."[1] Why do we derive more hope from the former than the latter?

3. **The Bible begins with God because God is the beginning and end. The world doesn't revolve around us, and neither does God.** God is radically God-centered. How does this reframe your understanding of your life, relationships, and vocation?

4. **God is not just a chapter in the story of your life; he's the author of your story, the one who makes sense of all the chapters of your life.** How does recognizing that our purpose is to align with God's design influence your decisions and actions in everyday life?

5. **Creation is the theater of his glory.** Reflect on how seeing creation as the theater of God's glory can enhance your appreciation for the natural world and deepen your worship of the Creator.

SCRIPTURES TO PONDER

What do these Scriptures about creation tell us about God and his character?

- **Genesis 1:1:** "In the beginning God created the heavens and the earth."

- **Psalm 19:1:** "The heavens declare the glory of God, and the expanse proclaims the work of his hands."

- **Colossians 1:16-17:** "Everything was created by him, in heaven and on earth, the visible and the invisible, whether thrones or dominions or rulers or authorities—all things have been created through him and for him. He is before all things, and by him all things hold together."

PRAYER FROM CHURCH HISTORY

Most high, all-powerful, righteous Lord, to you be all praise, glory, honor, and blessing. Praise be to you, my Lord, for all your creatures, above all Brother Sun, who gives us the light of day. He is beautiful and radiant with great splendor, and so is like you most high Lord. Praise be to you, my Lord, for Sister Moon and the stars. In heaven you fashioned them, clear and precious and beautiful. I praise and bless you, Lord, and I give thanks to you, and I will serve you in all humility.

—FRANCIS OF ASSISI (1182–1226)[2]

What Is the Unseen World?

ANSWER

The physical world is not all there is. The Bible describes an unseen realm of spiritual realities, with angels and demons engaged in cosmic struggle over God's plan of redemption.

SUMMARY

The Bible reveals an unseen realm of spiritual realities, where angels and demons engage in a cosmic struggle over God's plan of redemption. While Western culture often assumes that the physical world is all there is, many people throughout history and around the world accept the existence of a supernatural dimension. The Bible aligns with this perspective, asserting that reality extends beyond what can be seen and tested. This unseen world plays a significant role in the biblical narrative, influencing human history and revealing God's wisdom and plan through the church.

REFLECTION QUESTIONS

Content in bold comes from *The Gospel Way Catechism*, pages 39-40.

1. **The physical world is not all there is.** In what ways are you both comforted and challenged by this fact? What questions come to heart and mind when contemplating the reality of the unseen realm?

2. **The Bible describes an unseen realm of spiritual realities, with angels and demons engaged in cosmic struggle over God's plan of redemption.** What are some common ways that life in secular Western culture makes it difficult to believe this? How does our culture typically mask or hide this reality?

3. **In most places on earth, it's taken for granted that there is an unseen realm, where spiritual realities invisible to us exist and have real power.** When you were growing up, what views did your parents or grandparents have about angels and demons? How did their views align with or depart from what the Bible teaches about the spiritual world?

4. **In the early church, when new believers were baptized, candidates would renounce Satan and his works. Jesus taught his followers to pray, "Deliver us from the evil one" (Matthew 6:13).** Reflect on the biblical portrayal of spiritual forces at work in the world. How does this influence your understanding of good and evil, and the role of the church in God's plan?

5. **Reality extends beyond what can be seen, touched, and quantified.** How does recognizing an unseen realm change your perspective on faith and trust in God's sovereignty? Consider how this broader understanding of reality might deepen your faith and reliance on God.

SCRIPTURES TO PONDER

What do we learn about the unseen world from these Scriptures?

- **Ephesians 6:12:** "Our struggle is not against flesh and blood, but against the rulers, against the authorities, against the cosmic powers of this darkness, against evil, spiritual forces in the heavens."

- **Job 1:6:** "One day the sons of God came to present themselves before the LORD, and Satan also came with them."

- **Psalm 82:1:** "God stands in the divine assembly; he pronounces judgment among the gods."

- **2 Corinthians 4:18:** "We do not focus on what is seen, but on what is unseen. For what is seen is temporary, but what is unseen is eternal."

PRAYER FROM CHURCH HISTORY

May the strength of God pilot me, the power of God uphold me, the wisdom of God guide me. May the eye of God look before me, the ear of God hear me, the Word of God speak for me. May the hand of God protect me, the way of God lie before me, the shield of God defend me, the host of God save me. May Christ shield me today. Christ with me, Christ before me, Christ behind me, Christ in me, Christ beneath me, Christ above me, Christ on my right, Christ on my left, Christ when I lie down, Christ when I sit, Christ when I stand, Christ in the heart of everyone who thinks of me, Christ in the mouth of everyone who speaks of me, Christ in every eye that sees me, Christ in every ear that hears me.

—PATRICK OF IRELAND (FIFTH CENTURY)[1]

QUESTION 9
Why Did God Create Us?

ANSWER

God created us in his image to know and love him and share his joy. The good life is found not in inventing our purpose but in bowing to God's design and reflecting his glory.

SUMMARY

God created us in his image to know, love, and share in his joy. Unlike secular views that elevate humans to godlike status or reduce them to mere animals, the Bible teaches that our dignity is derived from being created in God's image. This grants us inherent worth and purpose. True fulfillment comes not from self-creation but from aligning with God's design. Our joy and identity are rooted in our relationship with God, reflecting his attributes and living according to his purpose.

REFLECTION QUESTIONS

Content in bold comes from *The Gospel Way Catechism*, page 42-43.

1. **We are images, reflections. The dignity of our humanity is derivative; it comes from him whose image we bear.** Our world says our meaning and worth comes from what we do. The Bible teaches that meaning and worth comes from the fact that God created us—it is inherent to who we are. Compare and contrast these two radically different visions of worth. Reflect on how exhausting it is to have to achieve our meaning and worth rather than simply receiving it as what God declares over us.

2. **We have worth and value not because of anything in ourselves, but because we are created in the image of God.** What are some common ways our culture makes meaning and value dependent on friends, likes, and status? How does the Christian understanding of value uniquely counter the popular cultural way of attributing value?

3. **God made us for relationship. He wants to be known.** How does knowing that our Creator desires to be known and enjoyed change the way we conceive of our purpose in life? Reflect on how the desire of God to be in relationship with us affects how we envision his posture toward us.

4. **We are not autonomous individuals, creating ourselves constantly by our decisions and choices; we are images, we are reflections.** How does this perspective challenge the modern view of self-creation and independence? Reflect on the limitations of self-reliance and the benefits of embracing our identity as God's creation.

5. **The good life is found not in inventing our purpose but in bowing to God's design and reflecting his glory.** How can you practically seek to live out God's design and reflect his glory in your daily life? Consider specific actions or attitudes that can help you align more closely with this truth.

SCRIPTURES TO PONDER

What do we learn about God's purpose for us in these verses?

- **Genesis 1:26-27:** "God said, 'Let us make man in our image, according to our likeness. They will rule the fish of the sea, the birds of the sky, the livestock, the whole earth, and the creatures that crawl on the earth.' So God created man in his own image; he created him in the image of God; he created them male and female."

- **Psalm 16:11:** "You reveal the path of life to me; in your presence is abundant joy; at your right hand are eternal pleasures."

- **Revelation 4:11:** "Our Lord and God, you are worthy to receive glory and honor and power, because you have created all things, and by your will they exist and were created."

PRAYER FROM CHURCH HISTORY

Lord, because you have made me, I owe you the whole of my love; because you have redeemed me, I owe you the whole of myself; because you have promised so much, I owe you my whole being. I pray you, Lord, make me taste by love what I taste by knowledge; let me know by love what I know by understanding. I owe you more than my whole self, but I have no more, and by myself I cannot render the whole of it to you. Draw me to you, Lord, in the fullness of your love. I am wholly yours by creation; make me all yours, too, in love. Amen.

—Anselm of Canterbury (1033–1109)[1]

QUESTION 10
Who Are We?

ANSWER

We are persons beloved by God, created to love God, love others, and care
for the world he has made. We become like what we love. Our identity
is found not by looking within ourselves but looking up to God.

SUMMARY

Human identity is often defined by achievements, self-expression, or societal roles. However, the Bible teaches that our truest identity comes from being created in God's image. This means we reflect his attributes such as love, creativity, rationality, and morality. Our worth is inherent, not earned. Understanding ourselves as image-bearers of God provides a firm foundation for purpose and value in life, calling us to live in a way that honors and mirrors our Creator.

REFLECTION QUESTIONS

Content in bold comes from *The Gospel Way Catechism*, pages 45-46.

1. **We become like what we love.** How does understanding yourself as an image-bearer of God shape your sense of identity and worth? Reflect on how this perspective influences your view of yourself and your intrinsic value.

2. **Our identity is found not by looking within ourselves but by looking up to God.** How is true identity found by looking up to God rather than within ourselves? How can focusing on Christ shape your sense of self and purpose?

3. **We are persons beloved by God, created to love God, love others, and care for the world he has made.** How does the concept of being an image-bearer influence your relationships with others? Reflect on how seeing others as fellow image-bearers of God can impact the way you treat and interact with them.

4. **Human identity is often defined by achievements, self-expression, or societal roles.** How does grounding your identity in God differ from the ways culture suggests we define ourselves? Examine

the differences between a God-centered identity and one based on societal roles, achievements, or self-expression.

5. **Understanding ourselves as image-bearers of God provides a firm foundation for purpose and value in life.** What practices can help you deepen your understanding and experience of being God's image-bearer? Consider spiritual disciplines, community involvement, and other activities that reinforce your identity in Christ.

SCRIPTURES TO PONDER

What do we learn about our identity from these Scriptures?

- **Genesis 9:6:** "Whoever sheds human blood, by humans his blood will be shed, for God made humans in his image."

- **Psalm 8:4-6:** "What is a human being that you remember him, a son of man that you look after him? You made him little less than God and crowned him with glory and honor. You made him ruler over the works of your hands; you put everything under his feet."

- **Colossians 3:9-10:** "Do not lie to one another, since you have put off the old self with its practices and have put on the new self, which is being renewed in knowledge according to the image of its Creator" (NIV).

PRAYER FROM CHURCH HISTORY

O crucified Jesus, in whom I live and without whom I die, mortify in me all wrong desires, inflame my heart with your holy love that I may no longer esteem the vanities of this world but place my affections entirely on You. Let my last breath, when my soul shall leave my body, breathe forth love to You, my God. I entered into life without acknowledging You; let me therefore finish it in loving You. O let the last act of life be love, remembering that God is love. Amen.

—RICHARD ALLEN (1760–1831)[1]

QUESTION 11
What Is Sexuality?

ANSWER

Sexuality is a God-given aspect of humanity. Male and female, our bodies are designed for procreation through the union of a man and woman in marriage. Sexuality is embodied, not imagined; physically grounded, not psychologically determined.

SUMMARY

In today's world, sexuality and gender are often seen as fluid and self-determined, but the Bible presents a different view. Sexuality is a God-given gift, expressed through the physical union of a man and woman in marriage, aimed at procreation and reflecting God's design. Our bodies are sacred, and sexual intimacy is both a physical and spiritual act meant for the covenant of marriage. This understanding of sexuality honors the differences between male and female, emphasizing that true fulfillment comes from aligning with God's purpose.

REFLECTION QUESTIONS

Content in bold comes from *The Gospel Way Catechism*, pages 48-49.

1. **"Nature made a mistake, which I have corrected."**[1]**–Christine Jorgensen.** Reflect on the cultural narrative that prioritizes self-perception over physical reality. How does this view contrast with the biblical teaching that our bodies are integral to our identity and designed by God for a purpose?

2. **"Your body is a temple of the Holy Spirit who is in you, whom you have from God"** (1 Corinthians 6:19). How does viewing your body as a temple of the Holy Spirit influence your understanding of sexuality and the importance of honoring God with your body?

3. **Sexuality is not just about personal fulfillment but reflects the covenantal nature of marriage and God's design for human flourishing.** How does this understanding of sex challenge the common view of sexuality as primarily about self-expression and personal pleasure?

4. **The church issues the most inclusive invitation in human history, welcoming people from every background, no matter their self-perception or struggle.** In what ways can you embody this

inclusive invitation while maintaining a biblical view of sexuality? How can you offer love and understanding to those with different views or experiences?

5. **In a world marred by sexual confusion, Christianity brings good news.** Reflect on how the biblical vision of sexuality can be good news in your context. How can you share God's good design for sex with humility and grace?

SCRIPTURES TO PONDER

What do we learn about God's design for sexuality from these Scriptures?

- **Genesis 1:27-28:** "God created man in his own image; he created him in the image of God; he created them male and female. God blessed them, and God said to them, 'Be fruitful, multiply, fill the earth, and subdue it.'"

- **Matthew 19:4-6:** "Haven't you read," he replied, "that he who created them in the beginning made them male and female, and he also said, 'For this reason a man will leave his father and mother and be joined to his wife, and the two will become one flesh?' So they are no longer two, but one flesh. Therefore, what God has joined together, let no one separate."

- **1 Corinthians 6:18-20:** "Flee sexual immorality! Every other sin a person commits is outside the body, but the person who is sexually immoral sins against his own body. Don't you know that your body is a temple of the Holy Spirit who is in you, whom you have from God? You are not your own, for you were bought at a price. So glorify God with your body."

PRAYER FROM CHURCH HISTORY

Blessed Trinity! Glorious unity! I deliver up myself to you. Receive me, write your name on me, and on everything I have. Set your mark on me, on every member of my body, and every part of my soul. By your grace, I resolve to walk in your way. I know my flesh will hang back. But in the power of your grace, I resolve to cleave to you and your holy ways—whatever the cost.

—JOSEPH ALLEINE (1634–1668)[2]

QUESTION 12

What Is Our Responsibility?

ANSWER

Our responsibility is to represent God by ruling wisely over his good creation, exercising authority in life-giving ways. We are called not to abandon or abuse our authority, but to serve as stewards.

SUMMARY

In today's world, the concept of responsibility often faces skepticism due to widespread abuses of power and authority. From government corruption to corporate exploitation, instances of misused authority are prevalent. This bias against authority is prevalent in Western culture, where many view power as a necessary evil at best. However, the Bible presents a balanced perspective, condemning abuses of power while affirming that authority and responsibility, when rightly exercised, are essential for human flourishing. Jesus exemplifies this balance as the Servant King, demonstrating that true leadership involves service and sacrifice. Our calling is to reflect God's good and loving nature by ruling wisely and serving others.

REFLECTION QUESTIONS

Content in bold comes from *The Gospel Way Catechism*, pages 51-52.

1. **We are called not to abandon or abuse our authority, but to serve as stewards.** What examples have you seen of people stewarding their authority well? What effect has their wisdom in leadership had on others?

2. **Our responsibility is to represent God by ruling wisely over his good creation.** We are responsible because we are made in God's image and given dominion over God's creation. In what ways do you rightfully step into the responsibilities God has given you? In what ways do you need to exercise the appropriate responsibility God has given you? Reflect on your work, possessions, your home, and your relationships.

3. **Jesus exemplifies this balance as the Servant King, demonstrating that true leadership involves service and sacrifice.** How does understanding Jesus as both a servant and a King reshape your view of authority and responsibility? Reflect on how this dual role challenges worldly notions of power. How does Jesus's example redefine how you use the authority you have in your own life?

4. **Human beings were created to rule. In our fallenness, that calling has been squandered.** Our fallenness reveals itself through the two equal and opposite errors of authoritarianism on one hand and passive withdrawal on the other. Which do you see most in your circles of influence? Reflect on what a restoration of responsibility would look like in those spaces.

5. **The King we worship chose a wooden cross for his throne. He came not "to be served, but to serve, and to give his life as a ransom for many"** (Matthew 20:28). How does Jesus's example of servant leadership challenge your current approach to responsibility? Reflect on steps you can take to align your leadership style with his.

SCRIPTURES TO PONDER

What do we learn about responsibility and stewardship from these Scriptures?

- **Psalm 8:6-8:** "You made him ruler over the works of your hands; you put everything under his feet: all the sheep and oxen, as well as the animals in the wild, the birds of the sky, and the fish of the sea that pass through the currents of the seas."

- **Mark 10:42-45:** "Jesus called them over and said to them, 'You know that those who are regarded as rulers of the Gentiles lord it over them, and those in high positions act as tyrants over them. But it is not so among you. On the contrary, whoever wants to become great among you will be your servant, and whoever wants to be first among you will be a slave to all. For even the Son of Man did not come to be served, but to serve, and to give his life as a ransom for many.'"

- **Romans 13:1:** "Let everyone submit to the governing authorities, since there is no authority except from God, and the authorities that exist are instituted by God."

PRAYER FROM CHURCH HISTORY

Lord, you have given our leaders the authority to rule by your magnificent and indescribable power so that we may comprehend the glory and honor you have given them, but also so that we may be subject to them, not fighting against your will. Lord, give them health, peace, harmony, and stability so that they might righteously oversee the stewardship you have given them. For you, Lord, heavenly, eternal King, grant to us (mere humans) glory, honor, and authority over the earthly creatures. You, Lord God, direct our plans according to what is good and pleasing to you so that when we righteously govern, in peace and gentleness, the stewardship you have given us, we may experience your mercy.

—CLEMENT OF ROME (DIED AD 99)[1]

What Is Work?

ANSWER

Work is the gracious expression of creative energy in response to God's calling.
We are to cultivate the world for the glory of God,
offering our skills to serve our neighbors.

SUMMARY

Work is often viewed as either a necessary evil or the source of our identity. The Bible redirects these views by teaching that work is a gracious expression of our creative energy in response to God's calling. From the beginning, humans were made for work. In Genesis, God commanded Adam and Eve to cultivate the earth. Thus, work is not a result of brokenness but part of God's purpose for humanity. Work should glorify God and serve others, reflecting God's creative nature and blessing. Our ultimate identity is found in being beloved by God, not in our productivity or job status.

REFLECTION QUESTIONS

Content in bold comes from *The Gospel Way Catechism*, pages 54-55.

1. **Work is the gracious expression of creative energy in response to God's calling.** Reflect on how viewing your work as a response to God's calling changes your approach to your vocation.

2. **From the beginning, humans were made for work.** Consider how this perspective on work aligns with the biblical view of work as a blessing and a calling. How does this change your attitude toward your everyday life as a Christian in God's world? Think of your chores in the home, family responsibilities, service in your community, etc.

3. **Work should glorify God and serve others, reflecting God's creative nature and blessing.** How does this quote challenge you to see the value in hard work and perseverance? Reflect on the biblical principle that work done for God's glory is never in vain.

4. **God commanded Adam and Eve to cultivate the earth.** Discuss how the concept of stewardship is central to the biblical view of work. What responsibilities do you have in your work environment to cultivate and care for God's creation?

5. **Our ultimate identity is found in being beloved by God, not in our productivity or job status.** Reflect on how this quote emphasizes the dignity and value of all work when done for God's glory. How does this influence your view of various kinds of work, both your own and others?

SCRIPTURES TO PONDER

What do we learn about work from these Scriptures?

- **Genesis 2:15:** "The LORD God took the man and placed him in the garden of Eden to work it and watch over it."

- **Ecclesiastes 3:12-13:** "I know that there is nothing better for them than to rejoice and enjoy the good life. It is also the gift of God whenever anyone eats, drinks, and enjoys all his efforts."

- **Colossians 3:23-24:** "Whatever you do, do it from the heart, as something done for the Lord and not for people, knowing that you will receive the reward of an inheritance from the Lord. You serve the Lord Christ."

PRAYER FROM CHURCH HISTORY

May my work be faithful; may my work be honest; may my work be blessed; may my work bless others; may my work bless you; may the wealth and work of the world be available to all and for the exploitation of none.

—CELTIC PRAYER[1]

QUESTION 14

What Is Rest?

ANSWER

Rest is when we cease from striving. Our hearts are restless until they rest in God our Savior and Sustainer. Living his way renews us physically and spiritually and provides a foretaste of eternal peace.

SUMMARY

In our busy, distracted world, many seek rest through various means, but true rest is found in God. Rest is more than a break from work; it is a state of being that orients us around God's will. From the beginning, God modeled rest by resting on the seventh day after creation. Rest is a form of worship and renewal, reminding us of God's provision and faithfulness. Jesus invites the weary to find rest in him, offering deep and abiding peace. This practice is countercultural, emphasizing our dependence on God and pointing toward the ultimate rest in God's eternal peace.

REFLECTION QUESTIONS

Content in bold comes from *The Gospel Way Catechism*, pages 57-58.

1. **Rest is when we cease from striving.** How does the concept of ceasing from striving resonate with your current approach to rest? In what ways can you incorporate true rest into your life?

2. **Our hearts are restless until they rest in God our Savior and Sustainer.** Reflect on times when you have experienced restlessness. How does finding rest in God address this restlessness?

3. **Living his way renews us physically and spiritually.** How can aligning your life with God's ways lead to physical and spiritual renewal? What changes can you make to live more in accordance with God's will?

4. **Jesus invites the weary to find rest in him, offering deep and abiding peace.** In what areas of your life do you feel weary? How can you respond to Jesus's invitation to find rest and peace in him?

5. **This practice is countercultural, emphasizing our dependence on God.** How does the practice of rest as taught in the Bible challenge the cultural norms of busyness and self-reliance? How can you demonstrate dependence on God through your practice of rest?

SCRIPTURES TO PONDER

What do we learn about rest from these Scriptures?

- **Genesis 2:2-3:** "By the seventh day God completed his work that he had done, and he rested on the seventh day from all his work that he had done. God blessed the seventh day and declared it holy, for on it he rested from all his work of creation."

- **Exodus 20:8-11:** "Remember the Sabbath day, to keep it holy. You are to labor six days and do all your work, but the seventh day is a Sabbath to the LORD your God. You must not do any work—you, your son or daughter, your male or female servant, your livestock, or the resident alien who is within your city gates. For the LORD made the heavens and the earth, the sea, and everything in them in six days; then he rested on the seventh day. Therefore the LORD blessed the Sabbath day and declared it holy."

- **Psalm 62:5:** "Rest in God alone, my soul, for my hope comes from him."

PRAYER FROM CHURCH HISTORY

Lord Jesus, you are light from eternal lights. You have dissolved all spiritual darkness and my soul is filled with your brightness. Your light makes all things beautiful. At night you give rest to our bodies. By day you spur us on to work. May I work with diligence and devotion, that at night my conscience is at peace. As I lay down on my bed at night, may your fingers draw down my eyelids. Lay your hand of blessing on my head that righteous sleep may descend upon me.

—GREGORY OF NAZIANZUS (329–390)[1]

QUESTION 15
What Is Freedom?

ANSWER

True freedom is submission to God. Freedom is not casting off all restraints and pursuing whatever we want. It is embracing the right restraints and aligning our wants with God's will, so we can pursue what is true and good and beautiful.

SUMMARY

In today's world, freedom is often seen as individual autonomy and the absence of external constraints. But the Bible teaches that true freedom involves submitting to God and aligning our desires with his will. This positive freedom allows us to pursue what is true, good, and beautiful. True freedom is not merely about doing whatever we want, but about wanting what is right and aligning our lives with God's purposes. Jesus's sacrifice set us free from sin, enabling us to live according to the Spirit and serve God fully.

REFLECTION QUESTIONS

Content in bold comes from *The Gospel Way Catechism*, pages 60-61.

1. **True freedom is submission to God.** How does this perspective challenge your understanding of freedom? Reflect on how aligning with God's will might differ from pursuing personal independence.

2. **Freedom is embracing the right restraints.** In what ways have you experienced greater freedom through embracing God's boundaries rather than resisting them? Can you identify a time when following God's guidance, even when it felt restrictive, led to a deeper sense of peace or freedom?

3. **Our ultimate bondage is our rebellion against God.** How does recognizing sin as bondage change your view of freedom and obedience? How is this different from the way the world portrays sin and freedom?

4. **True freedom is not found in following our desires but aligning ourselves with God's will.** What's a desire you're often tempted to follow that leads you away from freedom? Why does this definition of freedom sometimes feel counterintuitive to us?

5. **Jesus declared himself the long-promised liberator.** How does Jesus's role as liberator influence your understanding of freedom? Reflect on the significance of Jesus's sacrifice in setting you free to live according to the Spirit.

SCRIPTURES TO PONDER

What do we learn about freedom from these Scriptures?

- **Galatians 5:1:** "For freedom, Christ set us free. Stand firm, then, and don't submit again to a yoke of slavery."

- **John 8:31-32:** "Jesus said to the Jews who had believed him, 'If you continue in my word, you really are my disciples. You will know the truth, and the truth will set you free.'"

- **2 Corinthians 3:17:** "Now the Lord is the Spirit, and where the Spirit of the Lord is, there is freedom."

PRAYER FROM CHURCH HISTORY

Gracious Father, let your Holy Spirit take possession of my heart, that I may trust in you only, love you above all things, keep your commandments, and cling to you forever. Amen.

—MYLES COVERDALE (1488–1569)[1]

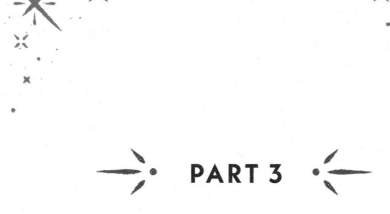

PART 3

Fall and Sin

What Has Gone Wrong?

ANSWER

The deepest source of misery in the world is not ignorance, injustice, or the failure to be true to ourselves. It is sin: cosmic treason against our Creator and his rule. Sin corrupts creation, wrecks relationships, and enslaves us to the Evil One.

SUMMARY

The fundamental problem in the world is sin—cosmic treason against God. Unlike theories that attribute the world's brokenness to ignorance, injustice, or failure to self-actualize, Christianity identifies sin as the root cause. Sin distorts creation, shatters relationships, and enslaves humanity to evil. This rebellion against God's rule results in widespread suffering and corruption, both vertically in our relationship with God and horizontally in our interactions with others. The Bible reveals that only God's redemptive plan can address this profound issue, offering a solution through Jesus Christ's sacrificial love and victory over sin.

REFLECTION QUESTIONS

Content in bold comes from *The Gospel Way Catechism*, pages 66-67.

1. **The deepest source of misery in the world is not ignorance, injustice, or the failure to be true to ourselves. It is sin.** How does this understanding of sin challenge the common secular explanations for the world's problems? Reflect on why it's crucial to recognize sin as the root cause of brokenness.

2. **Sin corrupts creation, wrecks relationships, and enslaves us to the Evil One.** How have the sins of those close to you impacted your own life and your own view of the world? In what ways have you observed the effects of sin in your own life and in the world around you? Consider how these effects manifest in various aspects of life and society.

3. **Sin is cosmic treason against our Creator and his rule.** Why is it important to view sin primarily as an offense against God? Reflect on how this vertical perspective influences your understanding of repentance and reconciliation.

4. **The world's understanding of sin focuses on the horizontal perspective, seen in individual experiences or institutional failures.** How can maintaining a Godward-oriented understanding of sin help address both personal and societal issues more effectively? Consider the implications of this perspective for social justice and personal growth.

5. **From Genesis to Revelation, the Bible is the story of God's overcoming love conquering our sin, Satan, and the world.** How does understanding the biblical narrative of sin and redemption shape your hope and outlook on the future? Reflect on the assurance and transformation that come from God's redemptive plan.

SCRIPTURES TO PONDER

What do we learn about the consequences and solution to sin from these Scriptures?

- **Genesis 3:1, 21:** "Now the serpent was the most cunning of all the wild animals that the LORD God had made. He said to the woman, 'Did God really say, "You can't eat from any tree in the garden?"'…The LORD God made clothing from skins for the man and his wife, and he clothed them."

- **Psalm 51:4-5:** "Against you—you alone—I have sinned and done this evil in your sight. So you are right when you pass sentence; you are blameless when you judge. Indeed, I was guilty when I was born; I was sinful when my mother conceived me."

- **Romans 3:23-24:** "All have sinned and fall short of the glory of God; they are justified freely by his grace through the redemption that is in Christ Jesus."

- **Romans 6:23:** "The wages of sin is death, but the gift of God is eternal life in Christ Jesus our Lord."

PRAYER FROM CHURCH HISTORY

Most merciful God,
we confess that we have sinned against you
in thought, word, and deed,
by what we have done,
and by what we have left undone.
We have not loved you with our whole heart;
we have not loved our neighbors as ourselves.
We are truly sorry and we humbly repent.
For the sake of your Son Jesus Christ,
have mercy on us and forgive us;
that we may delight in your will,
and walk in your ways,
to the glory of your Name. Amen.

—THE BOOK OF COMMON PRAYER

What Form Does Our Sin Take Against God?

ANSWER

We love God's gifts more than we love the giver of all good things. We push God from the center and place our trust in ourselves and other created things—dishonoring his name, defying his Word, and disbelieving his love.

SUMMARY

Sin is more than a mere social construct or personal failure; it is cosmic treason against God. While modern views may reduce sin to a failure of self-actualization or social injustice, the Bible emphasizes that sin is a direct offense against God. It manifests as idolatry—loving God's gifts more than God himself, dishonoring his name, defying his Word, and disbelieving his love. This pervasive condition impacts every aspect of our being, causing separation from God, broken relationships, and widespread suffering. Understanding the depth and gravity of sin is essential to fully grasp the gospel and appreciate the salvation offered through Jesus Christ.

REFLECTION QUESTIONS

Content in bold comes from *The Gospel Way Catechism*, pages 69-70.

1. **We dishonor the name of God, defy his Word, and disbelieve his love.** Reflect on how your actions or attitudes might dishonor God, defy his teachings, or disbelieve his love. How does recognizing these specific forms of sin shape your repentance and reliance on God's grace?

2. **Sin is the attempt to push God from the center—to trust ourselves or look for happiness in something created rather than the Creator.** Identify areas in your life where you have tried to replace God with self-reliance or worldly pursuits. Reflect on the consequences of these actions on your spiritual health and relationships. How can you recenter your life around God's will?

3. **Our sin against God is not a one-time mistake but a pervasive and chronic condition.** How do you see this chronic condition of sin manifest in your daily life? Consider patterns of thought, behavior,

or desires that reveal this deep-seated issue. How does this understanding deepen your appreciation for the need for continual repentance and transformation?

4. **The most profound source of misery in the world is human sin—our rebellion against God and his rule.** Reflect on how this perspective on sin contrasts with common secular explanations for the world's problems. How does acknowledging sin as the root cause influence your approach to addressing issues like injustice, suffering, and personal struggles?

5. **We will never appreciate all we have been saved *to* until we first understand what we have been saved *from*.** How does understanding the gravity of sin enhance your appreciation for the gospel? Reflect on the significance of recognizing what you have been saved from and how this understanding can deepen your gratitude and commitment to living a transformed life.

SCRIPTURES TO PONDER

What do we learn about the nature of sin and its consequences from these Scriptures?

- **Isaiah 59:2:** "Your iniquities are separating you from your God, and your sins have hidden his face from you so that he does not listen."

- **James 4:4:** "You adulterous people! Don't you know that friendship with the world is hostility toward God? So whoever wants to be the friend of the world becomes the enemy of God."

- **Romans 1:25:** "They exchanged the truth of God for a lie, and worshiped and served what has been created instead of the Creator, who is praised forever. Amen."

PRAYER FROM CHURCH HISTORY

O Lord and Master, I am unworthy both of heaven and of earth, because I have surrendered myself to sin, and become the slave of worldly pleasures. Yet, since you created me, and since you can shape me as you want, I do not despair of salvation; but made bold by your compassionate love, I come before you. Receive me, dear Lord, as you received the harlot, the thief, the tax collector and even the prodigal son. You love all people, so pour out your love upon me. Lift from me the heavy burden of sin, cleanse every stain of unrighteousness from me, and wash me white with the waters of holiness.

—BASIL OF CAESAREA (330–379)[1]

QUESTION 18

What Form Does Our Sin Take
Against One Another?

ANSWER

We use each other, treating people like things, and things like people. We love ourselves more than our neighbors, diminishing them through dishonor and injury, lust and exploitation, falsehood and envy.

SUMMARY

Sin manifests in our relationships through dishonor, injury, lust, exploitation, falsehood, and envy. This relational breakdown is not merely due to external factors but originates from our rebellion against God, turning our love inward. Scripture teaches that our selfishness and self-centeredness lead us to treat people as means to an end, while elevating things and desires above others. Our relational conflicts become a reflection of our broken relationship with God and the sin in our hearts. Recognizing this reality, we can seek forgiveness, reconciliation, and restoration through God's wisdom and resources.

REFLECTION QUESTIONS

Content in bold comes from *The Gospel Way Catechism*, pages 72-73.

1. **We love ourselves more than our neighbors, diminishing them through dishonor and injury, lust and exploitation, falsehood and envy.** What are some different attitudes and actions that show up in these ways of sinning against other people? How do these examples illustrate the impact of self-centeredness on our relationships?

2. **Our sin against one another reflects our broken relationship with God.** How has this truth been evident in your experiences? Reflect on moments when you have felt the effects of others' sins against you. How have these experiences shaped your understanding of sin and its consequences?

3. **Scripture helps us see how our sin against others takes place both through external actions and internal attitudes.** How do internal attitudes like lust, anger, and envy lead to external actions such

as adultery, murder, and theft? Consider how addressing the root attitudes can prevent harmful actions and promote healthier relationships.

4. **When we push God out of the center, we naturally place ourselves and our desires above others.** How have you seen this play out in your life or in society? Reflect on specific instances where self-centeredness led to relational breakdowns. How can recentering God in your life transform your relationships?

5. **The Bible's diagnosis is stark, explaining the reason we suffer the effects of others who sin against us while also exposing the ways others have suffered when we've sinned against them.** How does this comprehensive understanding of sin and its effects help you pursue forgiveness and reconciliation? Reflect on practical steps you can take to seek forgiveness and restore broken relationships.

SCRIPTURES TO PONDER

What do we learn about the nature of sin and its impact on relationships from these Scriptures?

- **Exodus 20:13-16:** "You shall not murder. You shall not commit adultery. You shall not steal. You shall not bear false witness against your neighbor" (ESV).

- **Matthew 5:21-22:** "You have heard that it was said to our ancestors, Do not murder, and whoever murders will be subject to judgment. But I tell you, everyone who is angry with his brother or sister will be subject to judgment."

- **Ephesians 4:31-32:** "Let all bitterness, anger and wrath, shouting and slander be removed from you, along with all malice. And be kind and compassionate to one another, forgiving one another, just as God also forgave you in Christ."

PRAYER FROM CHURCH HISTORY

Merciful Lord, pardon all the sins of my life, of omission and commission, of lips, life and walk, of hard-heartedness, unbelief, pride, of bringing dishonor on your great name, of impurity in thought, word and deed, of covetousness, which is idolatry. Pardon all my sins, known and unknown, felt and unfelt, confessed and unconfessed, remembered or forgotten. Good Lord, hear; and hearing, forgive!

—PURITAN PRAYER[1]

QUESTION 19
How Does God Respond to Sin?

ANSWER

God is not a permissive grandfather who winks at sin, but a perfect Father of fiery love. He hates sin because it defies his righteous character, disrupts our fellowship with him, and defaces us—his beloved image-bearers.

SUMMARY

God's response to sin is rooted in his holy love. He does not wink at sin or minimize its effects but stands implacably opposed to it. Sin defies God's righteous character, disrupts our fellowship with him, and defaces us as his image-bearers. God's hatred of sin stems from his love for his glory and his creation. His wrath against sin is an expression of his undying love for his people, seeking their restoration and the eradication of all that destroys.

REFLECTION QUESTIONS

Content in bold comes from *The Gospel Way Catechism*, pages 75-76.

1. **God is not a permissive grandfather who winks at sin, but a perfect Father of fiery love.** What are some ways this mindset might influence your own attitude toward sin? How can recognizing God as a perfect Father of fiery love reshape your understanding of sin and its consequences? Reflect on how this perspective could change your approach to personal holiness and your relationships with others.

2. **God stands implacably opposed to sin because of his great love for his glory and the good of those he made in his image.** In a society where sin is often redefined or dismissed, what cultural attitudes do you think most obscure the seriousness of sin as God sees it? Reflect on how these attitudes might affect your own perception of sin. How can a deeper understanding of God's love for his glory and for humanity help you challenge these cultural narratives in your own life and in discussions with others?

3. **If God were to stand at a distance, shrugging at the defacement of the beloved persons he made in his image, passive in the face of evil destroying his good creation, we would question his love for all he has made.** Many in the secular West wonder why God allows for so much evil and suffering but then are also frustrated at the idea of judgment and hell to punish evil. Reflect on this dynamic. How might you be able to speak to people who are confused about this aspect of God's character?

4. **God hates sin because it represents a betrayal of his love and goodness.** How does understanding sin as a betrayal of God's love change your approach to repentance and seeking forgiveness? Reflect on the importance of recognizing sin's personal and relational impact on your relationship with God.

5. **Sin's consequences are many. It corrupts the whole creation, shatters relationships, and enslaves us to the Evil One.** How do you see the consequences of sin playing out in your life and the world around you? Consider specific examples where sin has caused brokenness and how acknowledging these consequences can lead to genuine repentance and transformation.

SCRIPTURES TO PONDER

What do we learn about God's response to sin from these Scriptures?

- **Psalm 51:17:** "The sacrifice pleasing to God is a broken spirit. You will not despise a broken and humbled heart, God."

- **Isaiah 59:2:** "Your iniquities are separating you from your God, and your sins have hidden his face from you so that he does not listen."

- **Romans 1:18:** "God's wrath is revealed from heaven against all godlessness and unrighteousness of people who by their unrighteousness suppress the truth."

PRAYER FROM CHURCH HISTORY

O Almighty and merciful Father, you pour your benefits upon us—forgive the unthankfulness with which we have responded to your goodness. We have remained before you with dead and senseless hearts, unkindled with love of your gentle and enduring goodness. Turn us, O merciful Father, and so shall we be turned. Make us with our whole heart to hunger and thirst after you, and with all our longing to desire you. Amen.

—Anselm of Canterbury (1033–1109)[1]

Why Do We Feel Guilt and Shame?

ANSWER

Guilt tells us we have violated God's Word. Shame tells us to hide from God and from each other. Deliverance comes not through our power to resist guilt and shame but through God's provision to remove their source—our sin.

SUMMARY

Guilt and shame, often dismissed as mere social constructs, are deeply rooted in our broken relationship with God. Guilt arises from violating God's moral law, highlighting our need for forgiveness. Shame results from our fallen state, pointing to our need for restoration. Christianity teaches that true freedom from guilt and shame comes through Jesus, who removes our sin and restores us to right relationship with God. Understanding guilt and shame as indicators of our need for God's grace helps us find healing and wholeness in him.

REFLECTION QUESTIONS

Content in bold comes from *The Gospel Way Catechism*, pages 78-79.

1. **Guilt tells us we have violated God's Word.** Guilt and shame often manifest in subtle ways, influencing how we see ourselves and interact with others. How do you recognize the presence of guilt and shame in your own life? Consider the impact these emotions have on your daily decisions and relationships. What steps can you take to confront these feelings honestly before God and seek his healing and forgiveness?

2. **Shame tells us to hide from God and from each other.** Have you ever met a person who was not affected by shame? What are the different ways people try to cover up, hide, or mask their shame?

3. **Deliverance comes not through our power to resist guilt and shame but through God's provision to remove their source—our sin.** Secular people often misunderstand both what is wrong and how things can be made right. What specific verses from the Bible clearly depict the problem and the

solution? In what ways do those verses counter the world's thinking on the problem and solution we face in this life?

4. **In a world that sees guilt and shame as burdens to avoid at all costs, Christianity teaches that a proper understanding of guilt and shame can catalyze personal growth and transformation.** How can acknowledging guilt and shame as indicators of our need for God's grace lead to personal growth and transformation? Reflect on how embracing God's forgiveness can help you move beyond these feelings to a deeper relationship with him.

5. **Guilt reveals our transgressions against God's perfect standard, while shame compels us to conceal our brokenness.** How can understanding the biblical perspective on guilt and shame help you address your sin in a way that looks to the Lord? Consider how you can apply this understanding to your life and relationships, seeking God's provision for true freedom.

SCRIPTURES TO PONDER

What do we learn about guilt and shame from these Scriptures?

- **Psalm 51:3-4:** "I am conscious of my rebellion, and my sin is always before me. Against you—you alone—I have sinned and done this evil in your sight. So you are right when you pass sentence; you are blameless when you judge."

- **1 John 1:9:** "If we confess our sins, he is faithful and righteous to forgive us our sins and to cleanse us from all unrighteousness."

- **Romans 7:24-25:** "What a wretched man I am! Who will rescue me from this body of death? Thanks be to God through Jesus Christ our Lord! So then, with my mind I myself am serving the law of God, but with my flesh, the law of sin."

PRAYER FROM CHURCH HISTORY

Behold, Lord, an empty vessel that needs to be filled. My Lord, fill it. I am weak in the faith; strengthen me. I am cold in love; warm me and make me fervent, that my love may go out to my neighbor. I do not have a strong and firm faith; at times I doubt and am unable to trust you altogether. O Lord, help me. Strengthen my faith and trust in you. In you I have sealed the treasure of all I have. I am poor; you are rich and came to be merciful to the poor. I am a sinner; you are upright. With me, there is an abundance of sin; in you is the fullness of righteousness. Therefore, I will remain with you of whom I can receive, but to whom I may not give.

—Martin Luther (1483–1546)[1]

QUESTION 21
What Is Suffering?

ANSWER

Suffering is the experience of physical, emotional, or spiritual pain—a mark of life in a fallen world. Suffering is real and mysterious, but never meaningless, because God makes use of suffering to shape our character and increase our faith.

SUMMARY

Suffering, an inevitable part of life in a fallen world, is a universal human experience. While various worldviews attempt to explain and respond to suffering, Christianity offers a unique perspective. The Bible teaches that suffering, though often mysterious and challenging, is never meaningless. God uses suffering to develop perseverance, character, and hope in believers. The gospel story assures us that God is not indifferent to our pain; he entered human suffering through Jesus, promising to be with us and bring ultimate healing. Understanding suffering as part of God's redemptive plan can transform our response and deepen our faith.

REFLECTION QUESTIONS

Content in bold comes from *The Gospel Way Catechism*, pages 81-82.

1. **Suffering is real and unavoidable.** What are the top three moments of suffering in your own life? What are the most acute pain points in your own family story? How have you responded to suffering and pain when you experience them?

2. **Suffering is never meaningless.** Have you been able to trace out specific good things that God was providing in your life by allowing you to experience pain and suffering? Are you able to identify aspects of God's character after a moment or season of suffering that you didn't know before? What steps can you take to trust God's promises, even when the meaning of your suffering isn't immediately clear?

3. **God knows what it means to suffer.** No other worldview, religion, or philosophy has a God who suffers like God did in Jesus Christ. Think about the uniqueness of Christianity. In what ways is this

a comfort and help to you when you suffer? How can keeping this fact more central in your mind shape the way you pray to God?

4. **Suffering produces perseverance; perseverance, character; and character, hope.** In what ways have you seen suffering produce positive changes in your character or faith? Reflect on specific instances when suffering has led to growth in your spiritual life. How can you encourage others to see their suffering through this lens?

5. **God promises to bind up our broken hearts and heal our wounds.** How does this promise influence your perspective on personal suffering and the suffering of others? Consider how this hope can sustain you during difficult times. How can you share this hope with those around you?

SCRIPTURES TO PONDER

What do we learn about suffering from these Scriptures?

• **Isaiah 53:3-5:** "He was despised and rejected by men, a man of suffering who knew what sickness was. He was like someone people turned away from; he was despised, and we didn't value him. Yet he himself bore our sicknesses, and he carried our pains; but we in turn regarded him stricken, struck down by God, and afflicted. But he was pierced because of our rebellion, crushed because of our iniquities; punishment for our peace was on him, and we are healed by his wounds."

• **Romans 5:3-5:** "Not only that, but we also boast in our afflictions, because we know that affliction produces endurance, endurance produces proven character, and proven character produces hope.

This hope will not disappoint us, because God's love has been poured out in our hearts through the Holy Spirit who was given to us."

- **James 1:2-4:** "Consider it a great joy, my brothers and sisters, whenever you experience various trials, because you know that the testing of your faith produces endurance. And let endurance have its full effect, so that you may be mature and complete, lacking nothing."

PRAYER FROM CHURCH HISTORY

Whatever is in the cup that you, Lord, are offering to me, whether it be pain and sorrow and suffering and grief along with the many more joys, I'm willing to take it because I trust you. Because I know that what you want for me is the very best, I will receive this thing in your name. I need pain sometimes because you have something bigger in mind. It is never for nothing. And so I say Lord, in Jesus's name, by your grace I accept it.

—ELISABETH ELLIOT (1926–2015)[1]

PART 4

The Story of Redemption

QUESTION 22
How Does God's Rescue Plan Unfold?

ANSWER

God called Abraham and promised to create a worldwide family of faith. He rescued the children of Israel, gave them the Law, and called them to be a light to the nations. Salvation comes not through human ingenuity but divine initiative.

SUMMARY

God's rescue plan begins with his call to Abraham, promising to make him the father of a great nation through which blessings would flow to the world. This divine initiative continues with the deliverance of Israel from Egypt and the giving of the Law to guide them in righteousness. The Bible emphasizes that salvation is not achieved through human effort but through God's grace and power, highlighting the importance of surrender and trust in God's plan. This understanding liberates us from the burden of self-achievement and invites us to rest in God's providential care.

REFLECTION QUESTIONS

Content in bold comes from *The Gospel Way Catechism*, pages 86-87.

1. **God's rescue plan begins with his call to Abraham (Genesis 12).** He doesn't seem like a great candidate for the work of God in his life—does he? Consider how God chooses the weak in order to shame the strong and the foolish to shame the wise (1 Corinthians 1:27).

2. **Salvation comes not through human ingenuity but divine initiative.** What are some specific ways you are tempted to "save yourself" through good works? How would a greater awareness of salvation by grace alone fuel your gratitude and thanksgiving to God?

3. **God called Abraham and promised to create a worldwide family of faith.** God clearly chose one person, but that was for the sake of the many. What other places do you see this pattern repeated in the Bible? Do you recall specific situations when you've seen this dynamic repeated in history? What does this reveal to you about the nature of responsibility?

4. **He rescued the children of Israel, gave them the Law, and called them to be a light to the nations.** How does the biblical account of Israel's deliverance and the giving of the Law shape our understanding of God's plan for humanity? Reflect on the significance of these events and how they reveal God's character and purposes. How do they inform your role as a follower of Christ today?

5. **Recognize the beauty of God's divine initiative.** In what ways can recognizing God's initiative in salvation bring peace and assurance to your life? Consider how understanding God's proactive role in your salvation can transform your perspective on challenges and uncertainties. How can this recognition deepen your trust in God's plans?

SCRIPTURES TO PONDER

What do we learn about God's rescue plan from these Scriptures?

- **Genesis 12:1-3:** "The LORD said to Abram: Go from your land, your relatives, and your father's house to the land that I will show you. I will make you into a great nation, I will bless you, I will make your name great, and you will be a blessing. I will bless those who bless you, I will curse anyone who treats you with contempt, and all the peoples on earth will be blessed through you."

- **Exodus 6:6-7:** "Tell the Israelites: I am the LORD, and I will bring you out from the forced labor of the Egyptians and rescue you from slavery to them. I will redeem you with an outstretched arm and great acts of judgment. I will take you as my people, and I will be your God. You will know that I am the LORD your God, who brought you out from the forced labor of the Egyptians."

- **Deuteronomy 7:7-9:** "The LORD had his heart set on you and chose you, not because you were more numerous than all peoples, for you were the fewest of all peoples. But because the LORD loved you and kept the oath he swore to your ancestors, he brought you out with a strong hand and redeemed you from the place of slavery, from the power of Pharaoh king of Egypt. Know that the LORD your God is God, the faithful God who keeps his gracious covenant loyalty for a thousand generations with those who love him and keep his commands."

PRAYER FROM CHURCH HISTORY

Who are we, good God, that you should show us this great mercy? Forgive us our unthankfulness and sins, and give us your Holy Spirit now to cry "Abba, Father!" in our hearts. Assure us of our eternal election in Christ, and reveal more and more of your truth to us. Confirm, strengthen, and establish us—so we may live and die as vessels of your mercy, to your glory and for the good of the church.

—JOHN BRADFORD (1510–1555)[1]

QUESTION 23

What Do We Learn from Israel's Sacrificial System?

ANSWER

No earthly system of sacrifice can fully atone for sin. We cannot get right with God by willpower or good works. We need a perfect mediator to represent us to God and represent God to us.

SUMMARY

The sacrificial system in Leviticus demonstrates the gravity of sin and the need for atonement. These sacrifices show the temporary provision for sin, the necessity of cleansing, and the concept of substitutionary atonement. This system points forward to Jesus, the perfect mediator who fulfills the requirements of the Law and offers himself as the ultimate sacrifice. True atonement and reconciliation with God are not achieved through human effort but through divine provision.

REFLECTION QUESTIONS

Content in bold comes from *The Gospel Way Catechism*, pages 89-90.

1. **Our sin is ultimately directed upward (against God); the solution must come from above, not from within.** How does society's tendency to downplay or redefine sin contrast with the biblical understanding that sin is ultimately an offense against God? Consider how cultural narratives shape your view of sin and whether these perspectives align with or contradict the Bible's teaching. In what ways does recognizing sin as an offense against God challenge your approach to embracing the salvation God provides?

2. **Leviticus reveals the severity of our sin problem.** How does the sacrificial system in Leviticus deepen our understanding of the gravity of sin and the need for atonement? Reflect on how the detailed instructions and rituals challenge modern ideas of self-forgiveness, self-redemption, or moving on from mistakes. What do these ancient practices reveal about the seriousness with which God views sin and the lengths required for true reconciliation?

3. **God reveals his heart—he wants to be with his people, to forgive our sins and cleanse us of unrighteousness.** How does knowing that God desires to forgive and cleanse us change the way

you approach daily struggles and failures? Reflect on how this understanding impacts your daily thoughts and actions as a Christian. In what ways can we express gratitude for Jesus's intercession and sacrifice in our daily lives?

4. **Sin contaminates everything. Leviticus even has a category for unknown sins (Leviticus 4:27-28).** Reflect on the concept of "unknown sins" and how it relates to our understanding of sin in our lives. How does acknowledging the pervasive nature of sin impact our reliance on God's grace?

5. **Understanding the gravity of our sin, God's holiness, and the price of atonement helps us appreciate our need for a Great High Priest.** How does the role of Jesus as our Great High Priest fulfill the sacrificial system's requirements and offer us a preview of the renewed world? Reflect on how this understanding deepens your appreciation of Jesus's sacrifice and your hope for the future.

SCRIPTURES TO PONDER

What do we learn about God's provision for atonement from these Scriptures?

- **Exodus 19:5-6:** "Now if you will carefully listen to me and keep my covenant, you will be my own possession out of all the peoples, although the whole earth is mine, and you will be my kingdom of priests and my holy nation."

- **Leviticus 16:30:** "Atonement will be made for you on this day to cleanse you, and you will be clean from all your sins before the Lord."

- **Hebrews 10:12-14:** "But this man, after offering one sacrifice for sins forever, sat down at the right hand of God. He is now waiting until his enemies are made his footstool. For by one offering he has perfected forever those who are sanctified."

PRAYER FROM CHURCH HISTORY

Almighty and everlasting God, you hate nothing you have made and forgive the sins of all who are penitent: Create and make in us new and contrite hearts, that we, worthily lamenting our sins and acknowledging our wretchedness, may obtain of you, the God of all mercy, perfect remission and forgiveness; through Jesus Christ our Lord, who lives and reigns with you and the Holy Spirit, one God, for ever and ever. Amen.

—*THE BOOK OF COMMON PRAYER*

What Do We Learn from Israel's Kings?

ANSWER

No sinner can fulfill God's intent for humanity to rule with perfect wisdom and righteousness over creation. Even the best kings of Israel failed this high calling. We need a perfect King to provide eternal protection and peace.

SUMMARY

The history of Israel's kings highlights the limitations and failures of human leadership. Despite their best efforts, even the most revered kings like David and Solomon fell short of ruling with perfect wisdom and righteousness. This underscores the need for a perfect King who can fulfill God's intent for humanity. Our deep longing for a righteous ruler points us to Jesus, the perfect King who brings eternal protection and peace.

REFLECTION QUESTIONS

Content in bold comes from *The Gospel Way Catechism*, pages 92-93.

1. **The pendulum swings from good rulers to tyrants, from political hope to disappointment. None of this comes as a surprise if we immerse ourselves in the unfolding story we find in the Bible.** Sometimes we feel let down and disappointed because we put too much trust and hope in people who did not deserve it. We feel the same at other times because people who should have been trustworthy end up disappointing us. This dynamic is clearly revealed in the Bible. Reflect on times and places you've seen this dynamic unfold in the Scriptures.

2. **One of the striking features of the Bible is its honesty about the failures of even the best of Israel's kings.** Can you recall specific situations where Israel's kings failed? What do these teach you about the inevitable failure of human leaders? How can you balance trusting in the leadership structures God has placed over you with holding a realistic view of the flawed human nature of a human leader?

3. **No sinner can fulfill God's original intent for humanity to rule with total wisdom and righteousness.** How does recognizing the limitations of human rulers help you understand the necessity of a perfect King? Consider how this shapes your view of Jesus as the ultimate ruler.

4. **Even the best kings of Israel fell short of this high calling, reminding us of our need for a perfect King to come.** What are some common ways people hope for a leader to come along and make everything right? Why do people often resist right leadership when it is provided? Think of a specific way you have been disappointed with a human leader. How does Jesus uniquely and specifically provide what human leaders cannot?

5. **We desire autonomy and self-rule, yet paradoxically, we often pin our hopes and expectations on flawed and fallible political leaders.** How do these paradoxical desires reflect our deeper spiritual condition and need for Christ?

SCRIPTURES TO PONDER

What do we learn about the limitations of human leadership and the need for a perfect King from these Scriptures?

- **Psalm 146:3-4:** "Do not put your trust in princes, in human beings, who cannot save. When their spirit departs, they return to the ground; on that very day their plans come to nothing" (NIV).

- **Isaiah 55:8-9:** "'My thoughts are not your thoughts, neither are your ways my ways,' declares the Lord. 'As the heavens are higher than the earth, so are my ways higher than your ways and my thoughts than your thoughts'" (NIV).

- **Jeremiah 23:5-6:** "'The days are coming,' declares the Lord, 'when I will raise up for David a righteous Branch, a King who will reign wisely and do what is just and right in the land. In his days Judah will be saved and Israel will live in safety. This is the name by which he will be called: The Lord Our Righteous Savior.'"

PRAYER FROM CHURCH HISTORY

O King of glory, and Lord of valor, our warrior and our peace, may you win victories in the world through us your servants, for without you we can do nothing. May your compassion go before us and come behind us; be with us at our beginnings, and at our endings. May your will be done in everything we do, for you are our salvation, our glory and our joy.

—ALCUIN OF YORK (735–804)[1]

QUESTION 25

What Do We Learn from Israel's Prophets?

ANSWER

No human philosophy can fully enlighten the mind or cure the heart. The prophets to Israel delivered God's message and pointed ahead to a divine prophet who would not only explain, but embody his Word.

SUMMARY

In a world that often relies on individual moral compasses and modern "prophets" for guidance, the biblical prophets stand out as unique messengers of God's truth. Unlike contemporary influencers, the prophets spoke with divine authority, delivering God's Word and calling people to repentance. They foretold future events and proclaimed God's truth for the present. The prophets' messages went beyond popular ideologies, challenging societal norms and pointing to Jesus, the ultimate prophet who embodied God's Word.

REFLECTION QUESTIONS

Content in bold comes from *The Gospel Way Catechism*, pages 95-96.

1. **Modern prophets usually cater to their audience's desires and preferences.** What are some popular voices or movements today that promise personal fulfillment or enlightenment? How do these messages reflect society's desires and preferences? Reflect on how these modern voices compare to the messages delivered by biblical prophets, who often spoke hard truths rather than popular opinions.

2. **The prophets spoke with authority, not based on personal opinions or cultural trends, but on behalf of God himself.** What does it mean for a message to have authority beyond personal opinion or cultural trends? How does this challenge the way we evaluate the voices we listen to today? Reflect on how the authority of the prophets, grounded in their role as spokespeople for God, contrasts with the often subjective nature of modern messaging. How can we apply the authority of the prophetic message to our lives today?

3. **They challenged people to live according to God's commandments and to pursue righteousness.** What are some specific cultural trends or messages that are at odds with the messages delivered by the Old Testament prophets? Reflect on the sins they called out and the comfort they offered to those willing to repent. In what ways can you embody a prophetic voice in your daily life,

challenging the status quo with God's truth while offering hope and restoration to those who turn back to God?

4. **We need more than human enlightenment; we need the light of God's divine revelation to illuminate our path.** How do the biblical prophets provide a necessary corrective to the self-centered philosophies prevalent today? Reflect on ways you can seek and share God's wisdom in a world that often prioritizes human opinion over divine truth.

5. **The Old Testament prophets pointed forward to the divine prophet, Jesus the Messiah, who would not only explain but also embody the Word of God.** How does Jesus fulfill and surpass the role of the Old Testament prophets? Consider how Jesus's life and teachings bring ultimate clarity and hope in understanding God's Word and will.

SCRIPTURES TO PONDER

What do we learn about the role and importance of prophets from these Scriptures?

- **Isaiah 6:8-9:** "Then I heard the voice of the Lord asking: Who will I send? Who will go for us? I said: Here I am. Send me. And he replied: Go! Say to these people: Keep listening, but do not understand; keep looking, but do not perceive."

- **Jeremiah 1:4-10:** "The word of the LORD came to me: I chose you before I formed you in the womb; I set you apart before you were born. I appointed you a prophet to the nations. But I protested, 'Oh no, Lord GOD! Look, I don't know how to speak since I am only a youth.' Then the Lord said to me: Do not say, 'I am only a youth,' for you will go to everyone I send you to and speak whatever I tell you. Do not be afraid of anyone, for I will be with you to rescue you. This is the LORD's declaration. Then the LORD reached out his hand, touched my mouth, and told me: I have now filled your mouth with my words. See, I have appointed you today over nations and kingdoms to uproot and tear down, to destroy and demolish, to build and plant."

- **Hebrews 1:1-2:** "Long ago God spoke to our ancestors by the prophets at different times and in different ways. In these last days, he has spoken to us by his Son. God has appointed him heir of all things and made the universe through him."

PRAYER FROM CHURCH HISTORY

Oh Lord Jesus, we ask that you would give us words by opening our mouths so that we may pull down the strongholds, destroy evil counsels and every height that exalts itself against the true knowledge of God, and bring into captivity every thought so that every single one might be obedient to you, for indeed, only the one who has been taken captive by you may be said to be truly free.

—JOHN CASSIAN (360–435)[1]

QUESTION 26
Who Is Jesus of Nazareth?

ANSWER

Jesus of Nazareth is the sinless Son of God, born of the virgin Mary. He is more than a teacher or moral guide. His words and works give us the true meaning of God's Law and a preview of God's promise to make all things new.

SUMMARY

Jesus of Nazareth, the sinless Son of God born of the virgin Mary, is more than a moral teacher or guide. The Gospels present him as fulfilling God's Law and embodying God's promise to renew all things. His miraculous works and profound teachings reveal the heart of God and provide a glimpse into the future restoration of creation.

REFLECTION QUESTIONS

Content in bold comes from *The Gospel Way Catechism*, pages 98-99.

1. **Jesus lived the perfect life we could not live.** We spend a lot of time thinking about the birth and death of Jesus but probably not near enough time thinking about the life of Jesus. Reflect on the perfect life of Jesus. Absorb the truth that he lived that perfect life in your place and as your substitute. How does this understanding influence your daily walk with God and your reliance on his grace?

2. **He didn't relax the standards but intensified them—holding up a pristine vision of perfect righteousness.** In the Sermon on the Mount (Matthew 5-7), Jesus preached a very high vision of what the Father requires in order to be reconciled to God. But then Jesus went on to perfectly live that standard, and his record is counted in the place of those who trust him. Reflect on this dynamic in the life of Jesus's teaching and living. In what ways does this stir your heart with gratitude for what God has done?

3. **In his healings and miracles, he showed what the world is like when God is King.** Reflect on the significance of these miracles in revealing God's power and compassion. Consider what these

miracles teach us about the nature of God's kingdom and its impact on our understanding of hope, healing, and justice in the world today.

4. **Jesus came to set people free _for_ something, to live according to the purpose that God created for us.** How does Jesus's concept of freedom challenge contemporary views of freedom as the absence of constraints? Reflect on how Jesus's vision of freedom impacts your understanding of living a purposeful life.

5. **The Gospels show that Jesus made massive claims about his identity.** What claims did Jesus make about his identity, and how do these claims differ from the views of many people in society? Reflect on how Jesus's identity as the Son of God influences your faith and relationship with him.

SCRIPTURES TO PONDER

What do we learn about Jesus from these Scriptures?

- **Philippians 2:5-8:** "Adopt the same attitude as that of Christ Jesus, who, existing in the form of God, did not consider equality with God as something to be exploited. Instead he emptied himself by assuming the form of a servant, taking on the likeness of humanity. And when he had come as a man, he humbled himself by becoming obedient to the point of death—even to death on a cross."

- **Hebrews 4:15:** "We do not have a high priest who is unable to sympathize with our weaknesses, but one who has been tempted in every way as we are, yet without sin."

- **John 1:14:** "The Word became flesh and dwelt among us. We observed his glory, the glory as the one and only Son from the Father, full of grace and truth."

PRAYER FROM CHURCH HISTORY

By the obedience of Mary,
Lord made flesh
Dwell among us.
By the understanding of Joseph,
Lord made flesh
Dwell among us.
By the song of the angels,
Lord made flesh
Dwell among us.
By your birth in a manger,
Lord made flesh
Dwell among us.
By the adoration of the shepherds,
Lord made flesh
Dwell among us.
By the worship of the wise men,
Lord made flesh
Dwell among us.

—CELTIC PRAYER[1]

QUESTION 27
What Happened on the Cross?

ANSWER

Jesus gave himself—not only as a martyr, but as the Messiah, the atoning sacrifice for our sins. His death in our place conquers evil, conveys God's love, and creates a cross-shaped people.

SUMMARY

On the cross, Jesus gave himself as the atoning sacrifice for our sins, not merely as a martyr but as the Messiah. Jesus is the sinless Son of God who took the weight of our sin upon himself, enduring the judgment and defeating evil. His death was a substitute for ours. Unlike a martyr who dies for a cause, Jesus died for the world. The cross is the fulfillment of Israel's story of redemption, revealing Jesus as the ultimate priest, King, and prophet, and offering us forgiveness and victory. The cross forms a new community marked by self-sacrificial love.

REFLECTION QUESTIONS

Content in bold comes from *The Gospel Way Catechism*, pages 101-102.

1. **Jesus took the weight of human sin upon himself.** How does this act of bearing sin and God's judgment alter your perspective on what it means to be forgiven? Reflect on the gravity of Jesus's sacrifice and how it redefines the concepts of justice, mercy, and love in your life. How might understanding this profound act of atonement shape the way you extend forgiveness to others and live in light of God's grace?

2. **Jesus's willingness to endure suffering and sacrifice for the sake of humanity contrasts with modern views on avoiding pain and seeking personal gain.** In what ways are you struggling right now as you seek to pursue Christ?

3. **Jesus's death gives us forgiveness and victory.** How does the reality of Jesus's sacrifice change the way you live daily? Reflect on how the cross shapes your perspective on forgiveness and victory in

your personal life. How can understanding the depth of Jesus's love inspire a deeper commitment to live for him, influencing your decisions, relationships, and actions?

4. **The cross marks out the formation of a new people.** How does the cross create a community of believers characterized by self-giving love? Reflect on how the cross unites believers and calls them to live out a cross-shaped life, serving others and displaying God's love in tangible ways.

5. **The cross is the fulfillment of the sacrificial system.** What is the significance of Jesus being both the Great High Priest and the ultimate sacrifice for sin? Consider how the sacrificial system in the Old Testament points to the necessity of atonement and how Jesus fulfills this once and for all.

SCRIPTURES TO PONDER

What do we learn about Jesus's sacrifice from these Scriptures?

- **Isaiah 53:4-6:** "He himself bore our sicknesses, and he carried our pains; but we in turn regarded him stricken, struck down by God, and afflicted. But he was pierced because of our rebellion, crushed because of our iniquities; punishment for our peace was on him, and we are healed by his wounds. We all went astray like sheep; we all have turned to our own way; and the LORD has punished him for the iniquity of us all."

- **Romans 5:8:** "God proves his own love for us in that while we were still sinners, Christ died for us."

- **1 Peter 2:24:** "He himself bore our sins in his body on the tree; so that, having died to sins, we might live for righteousness. By his wounds you have been healed."

PRAYER FROM CHURCH HISTORY

Almighty God, whose dear Son went not up to joy but first he suffered pain, and entered not into glory before he was crucified: Mercifully grant that we, walking in the way of the cross, may find it none other than the way of life and peace; through Jesus Christ your Son our Lord, who lives and reigns with you and the Holy Spirit, one God, for ever and ever. Amen.

—*The Book of Common Prayer*

What Happened on Easter?

ANSWER

Jesus rose from the grave, bodily and visibly, in triumph over sin and death to launch God's new creation. The resurrection of Jesus is not a fairy tale, but the true story of his victory.

SUMMARY

The resurrection of Jesus is the cornerstone of Christian faith. It is not a myth or fairy tale but a historical event where Jesus triumphantly rose from the dead. This event launched God's new creation, showing that death is not the end and that God's redemption includes the renewal of our physical bodies. Jesus's resurrection offers hope and purpose, affirming the value of the human body and the promise of eternal life.

REFLECTION QUESTIONS

Content in bold comes from *The Gospel Way Catechism*, pages 104-105.

1. **The resurrection of Jesus *bodily* means that God is redeeming and restoring his creation. The physical world is not less-than or inferior to the spiritual.** How does the victory of Jesus over death motivate you to share the hope of the gospel with others? Reflect on how the promise of eternal life through Jesus's resurrection affects your priorities and goals. How does the resurrection challenge societal views on legacy and the meaning of life?

2. **God is redeeming and restoring his creation.** In what ways does this challenge or affirm your view of your body, culture, and the world?

3. Jesus's resurrection influences your actions. How does the reality of the resurrection give you purpose and endurance in facing challenges and uncertainties in life? How does it encourage you to prioritize eternal values over temporary concerns?

4. **Resurrection is the beginning of God's new creation.** How does the resurrection signify the start of something new rather than just the end of Jesus's earthly life? Reflect on the idea that the resurrection is not just the conclusion of Jesus's story but the beginning of God's new creation. How does this change your perspective on the future and the world around you?

5. The resurrection fulfills the deep human longing for restoration. How does the resurrection of Jesus fulfill the longings expressed in human stories and myths for restoration and triumph over death? Consider the parallels between the resurrection and the themes found in various myths and stories. How does knowing the resurrection is a true historical event impact your faith and understanding of God's plan for humanity?

SCRIPTURES TO PONDER

What do we learn about Jesus's resurrection from these Scriptures?

- **Romans 6:4:** "We were buried with him by baptism into death, in order that, just as Christ was raised from the dead by the glory of the Father, so we too may walk in newness of life."

- **1 Corinthians 15:20-22:** "As it is, Christ has been raised from the dead, the firstfruits of those who have fallen asleep. For since death came through a man, the resurrection of the dead also comes through a man. For just as in Adam all die, so also in Christ all will be made alive."

- **Philippians 3:10-11:** "My goal is to know him and the power of his resurrection and the fellowship of his sufferings, being conformed to his death, assuming that I will somehow reach the resurrection from among the dead."

PRAYER FROM CHURCH HISTORY

O God of my exodus, Great was the joy of Israel's sons when Egypt died upon the shore, Far greater the joy when the Redeemer's foe lay crushed in the dust! Jesus strides forth as the victor, conqueror of death, hell, and all opposing might; he bursts the bands of death, tramples the powers of darkness down, and lives forever. He, my gracious surety, apprehended for payment of my debt, comes forth from the prison house of the grave free, and triumphant over sin, Satan, and death. Show me the proof that his vicarious offering is accepted, that the claims of justice are satisfied, that the devil's scepter is shivered, that his wrongful throne is leveled. Give me the assurance that in Christ I died, in him I rose, in his life I live, in his victory I triumph, in his ascension I shall be glorified.

—PURITAN PRAYER[1]

What Does the Ascension Tell Us About Jesus?

ANSWER

Jesus is exalted as the true King of the world, worthy of ultimate allegiance. He intercedes for us before the Father and is present with us by the Spirit.

SUMMARY

The ascension of Jesus marks his exaltation as the true King of the world. Unlike human ambition that seeks self-promotion, Jesus's ascent follows his descent into humanity and death. Seated at God's right hand, Jesus intercedes for us, providing continual access to God. His ascension fulfills God's intention for humanity to reign over creation. We pledge allegiance to Jesus, whose kingship calls for humility and service. Despite ascending, Jesus remains present with us through the Holy Spirit, guiding and sustaining us in our journey of faith.

REFLECTION QUESTIONS

Content in bold comes from *The Gospel Way Catechism*, pages 107-108.

1. **Instead of grappling for positions of power and authority, seeking to one-up people as we climb the ladder of success, we follow in the steps of a King whose exaltation came after taking the lowliest place.** Reflect on how Jesus's example of humility and service provides a counternarrative to the self-centered ambitions often promoted in our culture. How does Jesus's model of humility before exaltation influence your understanding of leadership and success?

2. **Allegiance to the King.** How does acknowledging Jesus as King challenge cultural norms of independence and self-reliance? In what ways can your life better reflect the servant leadership of Jesus?

3. **Impact on priorities and values.** In what ways has Jesus's exaltation shifted your values? What does it mean to live with an ascension mindset? How can the reality of Jesus's ongoing reign influence your habits and attitude daily?

4. **Jesus's intercession.** How does the knowledge that Jesus intercedes for us before the Father affect your daily life and prayer? Reflect on the significance of having Jesus as our mediator and the assurance it brings.

5. **Presence through the Spirit.** How does Jesus's promise to be with us always through the Spirit impact your sense of his presence in your life? Consider how this promise shapes your understanding of God's closeness and guidance.

SCRIPTURES TO PONDER

What do we learn about Jesus's ascension from these Scriptures?

- **Luke 24:50-51:** "He led them out to the vicinity of Bethany, and lifting up his hands he blessed them. And while he was blessing them, he left them and was carried up into heaven."

- **Acts 1:9-11:** "After he had said this, he was taken up as they were watching, and a cloud took him out of their sight. While he was going, they were gazing into heaven, and suddenly two men in white clothes stood by them. They said, 'Men of Galilee, why do you stand looking up into heaven? This same Jesus, who has been taken from you into heaven, will come in the same way that you have seen him going into heaven.'"

- **Hebrews 4:14-16:** "Since we have a great high priest who has passed through the heavens—Jesus the Son of God—let us hold fast to our confession. For we do not have a high priest who is unable to sympathize with our weaknesses, but one who has been tempted in every way as we are, yet without sin. Therefore, let us approach the throne of grace with boldness, so that we may receive mercy and find grace to help us in time of need."

PRAYER FROM CHURCH HISTORY

Praise and thanksgiving be unto you, O God, who brought again from the dead our Lord Jesus Christ and set him at your right hand in the kingdom of glory. Praise and thanksgiving be unto you, O Lord Jesus Christ, you Lamb of God who has redeemed us by your blood, you heavenly Priest who ever lives to make intercession for us, you eternal King who comes again to make all things new. Praise and thanksgiving be unto you, O Holy Spirit, who has shed abroad the love of God, who makes us alive together with Christ, and makes us to sit with him in heavenly places, and to taste the good Word of God and the powers of the age to come. Blessing and glory, and wisdom and thanksgiving, and honor and power and might, be unto you our God forever and ever. Amen

—THOMAS F. TORRANCE (1913–2007)[1]

What Happened on the Day of Pentecost?

ANSWER

Jesus sent the Holy Spirit and ignited the global mission of the church. Through the Spirit's power, not our own, we spread the gospel to the nations as a people reconciled to God and to each other.

SUMMARY

On the day of Pentecost, fifty days after Jesus's resurrection and ten days after his ascension, the Holy Spirit descended upon Jesus's followers, marking the beginning of the global mission of the church. This event, with the Spirit's presence manifested as tongues of fire, symbolizes God's empowering presence within believers, enabling them to spread the gospel across cultures and languages. Unlike secular notions of power focused on personal achievement, the Spirit's empowerment emphasizes dependence on God, unity in diversity, and the mission to bring God's message of reconciliation to the world.

REFLECTION QUESTIONS

Content in bold comes from *The Gospel Way Catechism*, pages 110-111.

1. **At Pentecost, tongues of fire appeared over the heads of the believers present. Every follower of Jesus became a burning bush because God's presence was inside them.** How does this imagery of becoming a "burning bush" impact your understanding of God's presence in your life? Reflect on how this truth empowers you to live out your faith boldly and how you can make God's presence known through your actions and words.

2. **The gospel can enter a culture without erasing all its distinctives, and then challenge it, lift it, change it, redeem it, and bring it into a fullness it would otherwise lack.** How does the outpouring of the Holy Spirit challenge the world's emphasis on self-reliance and individual achievement? Reflect on how the gospel, while honoring cultural distinctives, calls us to depend on God's power rather than our own abilities. What practical steps can you take to consciously shift toward greater reliance on the Holy Spirit's guidance in your daily life and decision-making?

3. **The day of Pentecost represents the launch of God's global mission through the church, as the promise God made to Abraham to bless all the nations of the world through his descendants takes on a new shape.** How does the outpouring of the Holy Spirit at Pentecost, which united people from different cultures and languages, challenge the tendency toward division and cultural

separation in today's world? What value do diverse cultures and perspectives bring to the church body?

4. **The Spirit regenerates, sanctifies, gives victory over sin, teaches, unifies, and empowers our witness.** How does the Holy Spirit empower believers with different gifts for the common good? Reflect on the variety of spiritual gifts and their purpose in the church. How can you identify and utilize your spiritual gifts to serve others and glorify God?

5. **The Spirit creates profound oneness in the people of God, destroys barriers, brings peace, and fills us with the power to complete the mission.** How does the Holy Spirit's empowerment enable the church to fulfill its mission? Reflect on the ways the Spirit guides, teaches, and empowers believers to witness for Christ. How can you be more attuned to the Spirit's leading in your participation in God's mission?

SCRIPTURES TO PONDER

What do we learn about the Holy Spirit's work from these Scriptures?

- **Acts 2:1-4:** "When the day of Pentecost had arrived, they were all together in one place. Suddenly a sound like that of a violent rushing wind came from heaven, and it filled the whole house where they were staying. They saw tongues like flames of fire that separated and rested on each one of them. Then they were all filled with the Holy Spirit and began to speak in different tongues, as the Spirit enabled them."

- **Joel 2:28:** "After this I will pour out my Spirit on all humanity; then your sons and your daughters will prophesy, your old men will have dreams, and your young men will see visions."

- **Acts 1:8:** "You will receive power when the Holy Spirit has come on you, and you will be my witnesses in Jerusalem, in all Judea and Samaria, and to the ends of the earth."

PRAYER FROM CHURCH HISTORY

As a reconciled Father, take me to be your child; and give me your renewing Spirit, to be in me a principle of holy life, and light, and love, and your seal and witness that I am yours. Let him enliven my dead and hardened heart. Let him enlighten my dark and unbelieving mind, by clearer knowledge and firm belief. Let him turn my will to the ready obedience of your holy will. Let him reveal to my soul the wonders of your love in Christ, and fill it with love to you and my Redeemer, and to all your holy Word and works. Amen.

—RICHARD BAXTER (1615–1691)[1]

PART 5

Salvation by the Spirit

What Is Repentance?

ANSWER

Repentance is not merely regret over sin's consequences or our failure to live up to our standards. Repentance is turning away from evil—seeing sin in light of God's holiness and experiencing conviction in response to his kindness.

SUMMARY

Repentance goes beyond feeling sorrow or regret for our wrongdoings. True repentance is a transformative act of turning away from sin when we are confronted with God's holiness and kindness. It involves a deep conviction, a change of heart, and a reorientation of our lives toward God's kingdom agenda. It's not a one-time event but a lifelong process of aligning our lives with God's will. The gospel way emphasizes that repentance is a better way to live, marked by continuous transformation and dedication to God's standards.

REFLECTION QUESTIONS

Content in bold comes from *The Gospel Way Catechism*, pages 116-117.

1. **Repentance is not merely regret over sin's consequences or our failure to live up to our standards.** How does true repentance, rooted in recognizing sin against God, differ from merely feeling sorry for the outcomes of our actions? Reflect on ways that guilt or shame play a role in this process.

2. **Repentance is turning away from evil—seeing sin in light of God's holiness.** Do you think humility is a prerequisite to true repentance?

3. **Experiencing conviction in response to his kindness.** How has God's kindness led you to repentance? Reflect on specific instances where the awareness of God's kindness and grace has prompted you to turn away from sin.

4. **Seeing sin in light of God's holiness.** When do you still find yourself tempted to measure your sins against the sins of others rather than the holiness of God? How does this phrase correct a view of sin that's based on relativism?

5. **Turning away from evil.** What practical steps can you take to turn away from evil and align your life with God's kingdom agenda? Reflect on areas in your life where repentance is needed and how you can make changes that reflect true repentance.

SCRIPTURES TO PONDER

What do we learn about repentance from these Scriptures?

- **Psalm 51:10-12:** "God, create a clean heart for me and renew a steadfast spirit within me. Do not banish me from your presence or take your Holy Spirit from me. Restore the joy of your salvation to me, and sustain me by giving me a willing spirit."

- **Acts 3:19:** "Repent and turn back, so that your sins may be wiped out."

- **2 Corinthians 7:10:** "Godly grief produces a repentance that leads to salvation without regret, but worldly grief produces death."

PRAYER FROM CHURCH HISTORY

Lord Jesus Christ, you carry the lost sheep back into the fold in your arms, and delight to hear the confession of the tax collector—graciously remit all my guilt and sin. Lord, you hear the penitent thief, you have set a heritage of mercy for your saints, and have not withheld pardon from the sinner—hear the prayers of your servants according to your mercy. Amen.

—Johann Konrad Wilhelm Löhe (1808–1872)[1]

What Is Faith?

ANSWER

Faith is not based on our sincerity or the strength of our feelings;
it is not believing in ourselves. Faith is accepting the truth of the
gospel and entrusting ourselves to King Jesus alone.

SUMMARY

Faith, according to the Bible, is not about our emotional intensity or self-confidence. It is the acceptance of the gospel truth and a wholehearted trust in Jesus Christ as Savior and King. This faith is not self-generated but is a gift from God, leading us to depend entirely on Jesus for salvation. It is a better way, contrasting with the world's view of faith as a vague feeling or self-belief. The gospel way approach emphasizes that true faith is a trust in Jesus's finished work on the cross and his resurrection.

REFLECTION QUESTIONS

Content in bold comes from *The Gospel Way Catechism*, pages 119-120.

1. **Faith is not based on our sincerity or the strength of our feelings.** How does self-confidence fail us? In what situations have you relied on self-confidence only to realize that it falls short?

2. **Faith is accepting the truth of the gospel and entrusting ourselves to King Jesus alone.** Have you observed instances where people rely on the strength of their faith or sincerity for assurance rather than on Jesus himself? How does placing confidence in our emotions or efforts differ from truly entrusting ourselves to Jesus and his saving grace?

3. **Faith is accepting the truth of the gospel.** How does embracing the truth of the gospel change the way you live and make decisions? Reflect on how your daily life is shaped by trusting in the gospel's message, and consider areas where your faith could grow deeper in response to its truths.

4. **Entrusting ourselves to King Jesus alone.** How does this call to allegiance to Jesus challenge your daily life and decisions? Reflect on areas where you might struggle to fully trust Jesus and how you can surrender those areas to him.

5. **Faith is not believing in ourselves.** How does the gospel way of faith in Jesus confront the world's emphasis on self-reliance? Consider how this truth impacts your understanding of salvation and your day-to-day reliance on God's grace.

SCRIPTURES TO PONDER

What do we learn about faith from these Scriptures?

- **Ephesians 2:8-9:** "You are saved by grace through faith, and this is not from yourselves; it is God's gift—not from works, so that no one can boast."

- **Hebrews 11:1:** "Faith is the reality of what is hoped for, the proof of what is not seen."

- **Romans 10:17:** "Faith comes from what is heard, and what is heard comes through the message about Christ."

PRAYER FROM CHURCH HISTORY

My only comfort in life and death is that I am not my own, but belong—body and soul, in life and death—to you, my faithful Savior, Jesus Christ. You have fully paid for all my sins with your precious blood, and have set me free from the tyranny of the devil. You also watch over me in such a way that not a hair can fall from my head without the will of my Father in heaven; in fact, all things must work together for my salvation. Because I belong to you, my Messiah, by your Holy Spirit, you assure me of eternal life, and make me wholeheartedly willing and ready from now on to live for you.

—ADAPTED FROM THE HEIDELBERG CATECHISM[1]

QUESTION 33
What Is Union with Christ?

ANSWER

Union with Christ is our participation in the life, death, resurrection, and ascension of Jesus. Because Christ is in us, and we are in Christ, our identity is defined by our relationship with him.

SUMMARY

In today's world, identity is often based on external affiliations, career success, and social status. These markers can change and fail us. The Bible offers a better way through union with Christ, where our identity is securely rooted in Jesus's life, death, and resurrection. This union means we share in Jesus's story and are defined by our relationship with him. Unlike the unstable identities of the world, union with Christ provides a stable, lasting foundation. This union also leads to communion, where we experience an intimate fellowship with Jesus, transforming our lives and allowing us to live for God's glory.

REFLECTION QUESTIONS

Content in bold comes from *The Gospel Way Catechism*, pages 122-123.

1. **Our identity is defined by our relationship with him.** How does understanding your identity as rooted in your relationship with God affect the way you view yourself and your purpose? Reflect on how this perspective challenges cultural ideas of self-worth and how it influences your sense of belonging and direction in life.

2. **Union with Christ is our participation in the life, death, resurrection, and ascension of Jesus.** How does the concept of union with Christ transform your understanding of discipleship? Reflect on how being united with Christ in every aspect of his life shapes your daily decisions, struggles, and hopes for the future. How can this reality deepen your understanding of what it means to live as a follower of Jesus?

3. **Christ is in us, and we are in Christ.** Reflect on how this truth changes your sense of identity, security, and calling. How can you live more fully in the awareness of Christ's presence within you and your unity with him?

4. **Our identity is defined by our relationship with him.** How does the gospel way of union with Christ confront the world's emphasis on self-made identity and success? Reflect on how this union with Christ reorients your understanding of success and identity. How does this perspective provide comfort and assurance in the face of life's uncertainties?

5. **Union with Christ means you can now rest.** How does knowing that your identity is secure in Christ change the way you approach your daily life and relationships? Consider the freedom and peace that comes from resting in your union with Christ. How does this security affect your interactions with others and your overall outlook on life?

SCRIPTURES TO PONDER

What do we learn about union with Christ from these Scriptures?

- **John 15:5:** "I am the vine; you are the branches. The one who remains in me and I in him produces much fruit, because you can do nothing without me."

- **Galatians 2:20:** "I have been crucified with Christ, and I no longer live, but Christ lives in me. The life I now live in the body, I live by faith in the Son of God, who loved me and gave himself for me."

- **Ephesians 2:4-6:** "God, who is rich in mercy, because of his great love that he had for us, made us alive with Christ even though we were dead in trespasses. You are saved by grace! He also raised us up with him and seated us with him in the heavens in Christ Jesus."

PRAYER FROM CHURCH HISTORY

Sweetest Jesus, bind me with those bonds that held you fast, the chains of love. Allow that holy union to dissolve the cords of vanity and confine the bold pretensions of usurping passions. Imprison all the extravagancies of an impertinent spirit and lead sin captive to the dominion of grace and sanctified reason so that I may imitate all the parts of your holy passion. Allow me by your chains to get my freedom. By your kiss, enkindle love. By the touch of your hand and the breath of your mouth, cure all my wounds and restore the integrity of a holy penitent one and the purities of innocence so that I may love you and please you and live with you forever, oh holy and sweetest Jesus. Amen.

—JEREMY TAYLOR (1613–1667)[1]

What Is Justification?

ANSWER

Justification is God's declaration of righteousness for all who are united to Christ through faith: his life, death, and resurrection are counted as ours. We do not earn our entry into the family of God but stand before him faultless, by faith alone.

SUMMARY

The human heart naturally leans toward moralism, believing we must earn our way to goodness and approval. This self-justification fails, as cultures and standards shift, and our efforts never fully cover our guilt. The Bible presents a better way through God's justification, where we are declared righteous not by our works but by grace through faith in Jesus Christ. This "great exchange" means Jesus took our sin and gave us his righteousness. Justification is a divine gift, removing any grounds for boasting and offering us a secure identity in Christ. We stand faultless before God, not by our merits, but by faith alone.

REFLECTION QUESTIONS

Content in bold comes from *The Gospel Way Catechism*, pages 125-126.

1. **Justification is God's declaration of righteousness.** Our modern culture says you need to work hard to create, achieve, and promote an identity for yourself. Christianity says identity is not achieved but received. How does this truth of justification by faith shift your perspective on true validation and acceptance?

2. **We do not earn our entry into the family of God.** Reflect on how this truth challenges the mindset of striving for validation through good works. How does embracing justification as a gift from God rather than something to be earned affect your sense of security and peace? How can this truth reshape your relationship and interactions, leading you to extend grace to others?

3. **Stand before him faultless, by faith alone.** Whether before you came to Christ or after, what are some ways you've tried to build a name or identity for yourself? How did this effort make you feel? No matter how hard we try, we know something is lacking and our guilt and shame won't go away.

Only Christianity offers a way of standing before God that depends entirely on the work of another. How does this affect your view of yourself? How does this change how you approach God?

4. **His life, death, and resurrection are counted as ours.** How does this "great exchange" of our sin for Christ's righteousness shape your understanding of salvation and grace? Reflect on the significance of Jesus's sacrifice and how it changes your view of your worth and identity in God's eyes.

5. **We are united to Christ through faith.** How does union with Christ through faith affect your daily life and decisions? Consider how this union provides a foundation for living out your faith. What practical steps can you take to deepen your reliance on Christ's righteousness rather than your own efforts?

SCRIPTURES TO PONDER

What do we learn about justification from these Scriptures?

- **Romans 3:24:** "They are justified freely by his grace through the redemption that is in Christ Jesus."

- **2 Corinthians 5:21:** "He made the one who did not know sin to be sin for us, so that in him we might become the righteousness of God."

- **Ephesians 2:8-9:** "You are saved by grace through faith, and this is not from yourselves; it is God's gift—not from works, so that no one can boast."

PRAYER FROM CHURCH HISTORY

Oh, the surpassing kindness and love of God! You did not hate or reject or bear a grudge against us but you were patient and bore with us…you yourself gave your own Son, a ransom on our behalf, the Holy for the lawless, the innocent for the guilty, the righteous for the unrighteous, the incorruptible for the corruptible, the immortal for the mortal. Oh, the sweet exchange! Oh, the fathomless creation! Oh, the unexpected benefits that the lawlessness of many should be concealed in the one righteous, and the righteousness of the one should justify many lawless.

—THE EPISTLE TO DIOGNETUS (2ND CENTURY)[1]

QUESTION 35
What Is Sanctification?

ANSWER
Sanctification is the work of the Spirit to make us more and more like Jesus. It is not the pursuit of just being yourself but the project of growing with others in the righteousness God imparts to his people.

SUMMARY
In a world obsessed with self-improvement and personal branding, sanctification offers a better way—grounded not in self-effort but in God's transformative work through the Holy Spirit. Sanctification is the process of becoming more like Jesus, involving heart change that leads to outward transformation. Unlike the isolating and competitive pursuit of personal perfection, Christian sanctification happens within a community, fostering mutual growth and support. It shifts the focus from self-centered ambitions to God's eternal purposes, emphasizing inner renewal and collective righteousness over individual achievements.

REFLECTION QUESTIONS
Content in bold comes from *The Gospel Way Catechism*, pages 128-129.

1. **It is not the pursuit of just being yourself but the project of growing with others.** Reflect on the ways in which striving to shape your own image has influenced your spiritual journey. What shifts might take place if you were to focus on growing in Christlikeness rather than chasing a self-defined ideal? How can embracing the community of believers help you in this transformative process?

2. **Sanctification refers to the process of being made holy, or more specifically, becoming more like Jesus.** How does sanctification shape the way you understand self-improvement? What is God's role and your role in becoming more like Jesus?

3. **Growing with others in the righteousness God imparts to his people.** Self-improvement can feel competitive, where we not only try to be the best version of ourselves but we try to be better than those around us. Christianity offers a different way of becoming a better person. We don't compete with one another to do better; instead, we rely on the Spirit's work in our lives to shape us into the image of Jesus. Instead of trying to outperform one another, we can support and encourage one

another. In what ways does this view of self-improvement provide comfort? How can you help others become more like Jesus?

4. **Sanctification involves a profound inner transformation.** How does this inner transformation differ from surface-level changes driven by comparison culture and trends? Reflect on the difference between outward behaviors and inward heart change. How can you prioritize heart transformation in your daily practices?

5. **The Spirit shapes our attitudes and motives.** What practical steps can you take to abide in Jesus and allow the Holy Spirit to shape your attitudes and motives? Consider incorporating spiritual disciplines and practices that align your heart with the Spirit's work. How can you cultivate a life that reflects Jesus's character?

SCRIPTURES TO PONDER

What do we learn about sanctification from these Scriptures?

- **Romans 12:2:** "Do not be conformed to this age, but be transformed by the renewing of your mind, so that you may discern what is the good, pleasing, and perfect will of God."

- **Philippians 1:6:** "I am sure of this, that he who started a good work in you will carry it on to completion until the day of Christ Jesus."

- **2 Corinthians 3:18:** "We all, with unveiled faces, are looking as in a mirror at the glory of the Lord and are being transformed into the same image from glory to glory; this is from the Lord who is the Spirit."

PRAYER FROM CHURCH HISTORY

O Lord my God, instruct my ignorance and enlighten my darkness. You are my King, take possession of all my powers and abilities and let me be no longer under the dominion of sin. Give me a sincere and heartfelt repentance for all my offenses and strengthen by your grace my resolution to amend my ways. Grant me also the spirit of prayer and supplication according to your own most gracious promises.

—PHILLIS WHEATLEY (1753–1784)[1]

QUESTION 36

What Is Glorification?

ANSWER

Glorification is the Spirit's ultimate work, resurrecting us into eternal splendor as we are fully transformed into the likeness of Jesus. Our hope for immortality rests in God's promise, not human plans.

SUMMARY

In a world obsessed with transcending human limitations through technology, glorification offers a better way—God's way. Glorification is the final act of the Holy Spirit, transforming us into the likeness of Jesus and resurrecting us into eternal splendor. Unlike human pursuits of immortality, which rely on self-sufficiency and technological advancements, glorification is rooted in God's unchanging promises. It is the culmination of our sanctification journey, ensuring that we are perfected and fully conformed to Christ's image. Our hope for immortality rests in God's power and sovereignty, not in human ingenuity.

REFLECTION QUESTIONS

Content in bold comes from *The Gospel Way Catechism*, pages 131-132.

1. **The world is captivated by the quest for immorality through human ingenuity.** What are some ways people seek to escape or transcend this world and our present reality?

2. **Glorification is not about our feats but the faithfulness of God.** How is the biblical doctrine of glorification "a better way" of anticipating the afterlife compared to saving ourselves through technology and science?

3. **Our hope for immortality rests in God's promise, not human plans.** Many people want to live forever, and they spend their lives trying to engineer this outcome. What are some typical ways people try to prolong their lives and guard against death? How does the promise of glorification through the Holy Spirit contrast with these different visions of life?

4. **Fully transformed into the likeness of Jesus.** Think about the relationship between sanctification and glorification. What's one area in your life that offers you an opportunity to better conform to the image of Christ?

5. **The Spirit's ultimate work, resurrecting us into eternal splendor.** What ways does the story of deliverance through technology simply not work? What promises does it make that it can't keep? How is the promise of the Holy Spirit transforming us and eventually delivering us good news compared to the story of deliverance through technology?

SCRIPTURES TO PONDER

What do we learn about glorification from these Scriptures?

- **Romans 8:29-30:** "Those he foreknew he also predestined to be conformed to the image of his Son, so that he would be the firstborn among many brothers and sisters. And those he predestined, he also called; and those he called, he also justified; and those he justified, he also glorified."

- **1 Corinthians 15:42-44:** "It is with the resurrection of the dead: Sown in corruption, raised in incorruption; sown in dishonor, raised in glory; sown in weakness, raised in power; sown a natural body, raised a spiritual body. If there is a natural body, there is also a spiritual body."

- **1 John 3:2:** "Dear friends, we are God's children now, and what we will be has not yet been revealed. We know that when he appears, we will be like him because we will see him as he is."

PRAYER FROM CHURCH HISTORY

Eternal God and dear Father, teach me as your poor, unworthy child to keep to your ways and paths. This is my sincere desire, that through your power I may press even unto death, through all sorrows, sufferings, anguish, and pain. Increase our love and faith, and comfort us by your holy word, in which we may firmly trust.

—Anna of Freiburg (died 1529)[1]

PART 6

The People of God

What Is the Kingdom of God?

ANSWER

The kingdom of God is the redemptive rule of God through his people over his creation—a reign already present, though not yet in fullness. We do not build the kingdom; yet by grace we are drawn into the work of God to remake the world under Jesus the King.

SUMMARY

The kingdom of God is God's redemptive rule over creation through his people, already present but not yet fully realized. Our culture often seeks political leaders or systems to enact justice, but the Bible offers a vision beyond earthly kingdoms. While we don't build or bring the kingdom ourselves, we are called to participate in God's work of renewal under King Jesus. The kingdom was inaugurated through Jesus's life and ministry and will be fully realized upon his return. True participation in the kingdom requires allegiance to Jesus as King, not just appreciation for its cultural benefits.

REFLECTION QUESTIONS

Content in bold comes from *The Gospel Way Catechism*, pages 136-137.

1. **The kingdom of God is the redemptive rule of God through his people over his creation.** Consider the different times and places the kingdom of God is present throughout the Bible. What does the presence of the kingdom of God in the Old Testament teach us about the centrality of this theme in the Scriptures? Is the kingdom of God a new idea or an old idea in the Bible?

2. **We do not build the kingdom; yet by grace we are drawn into the work of God to remake the world under Jesus the King.** How does this definition of the kingdom challenge the way you already view serving God and doing justice in the world? In what ways does it challenge your view?

3. **There is an "already, not yet" tension that characterizes the kingdom.** What is some clear evidence of the fact that the kingdom of God is already here? Correspondingly, what is some evidence that the kingdom is not yet fully here?

4. **Jesus told his followers to seek his kingdom first (Matthew 6:33).** How does seeking first the kingdom of God influence your priorities and decision-making? Reflect on the ways your life changes when you prioritize God's kingdom above all else. How does this shift impact your daily actions and long-term goals?

5. **We are always in search of a new agenda, a new class of leaders, new laws that will enact justice and peace.** How does the kingdom of God address our longing for justice and peace differently than political systems? Consider how the gospel way offers a more profound solution to the world's problems. How can you participate in God's kingdom work to promote true justice and peace?

SCRIPTURES TO PONDER

What do these Scriptures teach us about the coming of God's kingdom and our salvation?

- **Matthew 6:10:** "Your kingdom come. Your will be done on earth as it is in heaven."

- **Luke 17:20-21:** "When he was asked by the Pharisees when the kingdom of God would come, he answered them, 'The kingdom of God is not coming with something observable; no one will say, "See here!" or "There!" For you see, the kingdom of God is in your midst.'"

- **Colossians 1:13-14:** "He has rescued us from the domain of darkness and transferred us into the kingdom of the Son he loves. In him we have redemption, the forgiveness of sins."

PRAYER FROM CHURCH HISTORY

I am no longer my own, but yours. Put me in any place of service, rank me with any type of people; put me to work, put me to suffering. Let me be useful for you or laid aside for you, exalted for you or brought low by you. Let me be full, let me be empty. Let me have all things, let me have nothing. I freely and heartily yield all things to your pleasure and for your use.

—JOHN WESLEY (1703–1791)[1]

What Is the Church?

ANSWER

The church is the people of God—established by the gospel and chosen by grace. It is not a religious club or social action group. The church comes together to be a local embassy, a picture of God's kingdom through worship and love.

SUMMARY

The church is not just a social group or a gathering of like-minded people—it is the people of God, formed by the gospel and chosen by grace. The church serves as an outpost of God's kingdom, displaying his love and grace through worship and service. Far from being optional, the church is essential to Christian life, where believers grow together in community, love, and accountability. The church is a signpost, pointing back to the cross and forward to the coming kingdom of God. It is a holy priesthood, called to offer spiritual worship and proclaim God's glory to the world.

REFLECTION QUESTIONS

Content in bold comes from *The Gospel Way Catechism*, pages 139-140.

1. **The church is the people of God—established by the gospel and chosen by grace.** Think about the ways this definition provides great humility and great dignity. Reflect on the humble state of our souls in that we had to be chosen by grace. Think further on the character of God in that he wanted to save you. Journal your thoughts.

2. **Through words and works of love, the church showcases God's grace, seen in our obedience as we make disciples, baptize them, and celebrate the Lord's Supper together.** While God is sovereign, he chooses to work through the everyday lives and activities of his servants. Think about the role God has given you in communicating the gospel to people. How is this an honor and responsibility to be stewarded well?

3. **The church is essential to the Christian faith.** How does viewing the church as essential influence your commitment and participation? Reflect on the importance of being actively involved in your church and how it aids your spiritual growth.

4. **The church is a local embassy, a picture of God's kingdom through worship and love.** Consider specific actions and initiatives that could help your church embody the values and teachings of God's kingdom. How can your congregation collectively demonstrate worship and love that reflects the reality of God's reign in your local context? Reflect on how these efforts might impact your church's relationship with the surrounding community.

5. **The church is a signpost pointing back to the cross and forward to the coming kingdom of God.** How does this perspective influence your view of the church's mission and your role in it? Reflect on how your actions and attitudes can help point others to Jesus and the hope of his coming kingdom.

SCRIPTURES TO PONDER

What do these Scriptures teach us about the identity of God's people and how we are to relate to one another and to the world?

- **Ephesians 2:19-21:** "You are no longer foreigners and strangers, but fellow citizens with the saints, and members of God's household, built on the foundation of the apostles and prophets, with Christ Jesus himself as the cornerstone. In him the whole building, being put together, grows into a holy temple in the Lord."

- **1 Corinthians 12:12-14:** "Just as the body is one and has many parts, and all the parts of that body, though many, are one body—so also is Christ. For we were all baptized by one Spirit into one body—whether Jews or Greeks, whether slaves or free—and we were all given one Spirit to drink. Indeed, the body is not one part but many."

- **1 Peter 2:9-10:** "You are a chosen race, a royal priesthood, a holy nation, a people for his possession, so that you may proclaim the praises of the one who called you out of darkness into his marvelous light. Once you were not a people, but now you are God's people; you had not received mercy, but now you have received mercy."

PRAYER FROM CHURCH HISTORY

We ask that you send the Holy Spirit as a holy offering to the holy church. As we assemble, give to all the saints the fullness of the Holy Spirit for the confirmation of true faith so that we may praise and glorify you through your Son, Jesus Christ, through whom glory and honor to the Father and the Son with the Holy Spirit in your holy church are yours now and forever! Amen.

—Hippolytus of Rome (170–235)[1]

QUESTION 39
What Is Baptism?

ANSWER

Baptism is the public sign of our salvation—an identity marker that reveals we are not our own but belong to the people of God. Baptism signifies our purification from sin and our participation in Jesus's death and resurrection.

SUMMARY

Baptism is a public declaration of our new identity in Christ, signifying our cleansing from sin and participation in Jesus's death and resurrection. In a world where identity is often shaped by politics, self-expression, or group affiliations, baptism offers a different foundation: we belong to God and his people. Baptism marks us as part of the kingdom of God, proclaiming that our true identity comes from him. Through baptism, we declare that we are not defined by self or society but by our union with Christ, leaving behind our old life and stepping into the new life we have in Jesus

REFLECTION QUESTIONS

Content in bold comes from *The Gospel Way Catechism*, pages 142-143.

1. **In baptism, we see the kingdom of God as our primary source of identity and God's people as our primary place for belonging.** What are some ways you are commonly tempted to identify with people, places, political parties, and other events in your life? Consider how baptism has influenced your sense of self in these situations.

2. **Baptism illustrates how Jesus has cleansed us from our sins on the inside.** What are some ways our culture argues that we need to be cleansed and healed? What does our world teach us about how wrong things can be made right?

3. **Baptism means our past has been buried, and our future has been reborn in Jesus Christ.** How does your baptism shape your understanding of your identity in Christ and your place in God's kingdom? Think about how the significance of baptism can serve as a daily reminder of your new life in Christ and your role as a member of God's family. How can this understanding influence your

decisions, actions, and relationships with others? Consider practical ways to live out your baptismal identity in everyday life, reflecting your commitment to God and his kingdom.

4. **It's not so much "I claim Christ" as it is "Christ has claimed me."** How does this understanding of baptism shape your daily walk with Jesus? Reflect on how acknowledging that Christ has claimed you can change your approach to faith and obedience.

5. **We're no longer just individuals; we're part of something much bigger.** How does your baptism connect you with the larger body of Christ? Reflect on the sense of community and shared mission that comes with being part of the church. How can you live out this communal aspect in your church and community?

SCRIPTURES TO PONDER

How do these Scriptures help us understand the meaning and significance of baptism?

- **Romans 6:3-4:** "Are you unaware that all of us who were baptized into Christ Jesus were baptized into his death? Therefore we were buried with him by baptism into death, in order that, just as Christ was raised from the dead by the glory of the Father, so we too may walk in newness of life."

- **Acts 2:38:** "Peter replied, 'Repent and be baptized, each of you, in the name of Jesus Christ for the forgiveness of your sins, and you will receive the gift of the Holy Spirit.'"

- **Galatians 3:27:** "Those of you who were baptized into Christ have been clothed with Christ."

PRAYER FROM CHURCH HISTORY

I believe in God, the Father almighty,
creator of heaven and earth;
I believe in Jesus Christ, his only Son, our Lord.
He was conceived by the power of the Holy Spirit
and born of the Virgin Mary.
He suffered under Pontius Pilate,
was crucified, died, and was buried.
He descended to the dead.
On the third day he rose again.
He ascended into heaven,
and is seated at the right hand of the Father.
He will come again to judge the living and the dead.
I believe in the Holy Spirit,
the holy catholic Church,
the communion of saints,
the forgiveness of sins
the resurrection of the body,
and the life everlasting. Amen.

—*The Apostles' Creed* (ancient baptismal declaration)

QUESTION 40

What Is the Lord's Supper?

ANSWER

The Lord's Supper is communion with King Jesus at his table with his people. We eat the bread and drink the cup, giving thanks for his body and blood, strengthened for service by this foretaste of the feast to come.

SUMMARY

The Lord's Supper is an intimate act of communion with Jesus, where we give thanks for his body and blood, receiving spiritual nourishment and strength. In contrast to the consumer culture that fosters dissatisfaction and the endless pursuit of more, the Lord's Supper satisfies our deepest hunger for grace and connection with God. Through the bread and cup, we remember Jesus's sacrifice, are spiritually renewed, and are drawn into a greater community of believers. The supper not only looks back to Christ's atoning work on the cross but also points forward to the future feast with him in eternity.

REFLECTION QUESTIONS

Content in bold comes from *The Gospel Way Catechism*, pages 145-146.

1. **The Lord's Supper addresses our spiritual hunger and profound discontentment.** How have you seen worldly solutions fall short? Are there any you have been tempted to believe would satisfy your own hungers? What are some of the obvious and less obvious ways you experience this in your life?

2. **When we gather around the Lord's table, we take our place as part of a larger community of believers.** Our individualistic society leads us to forget the fact that the Lord's Supper is a meal shared by the church as a whole. How does sharing the meal with the church as a whole enhance your sense of community and belonging?

3. **The Lord's Supper isn't merely a commemoration of a past event; it's a present source of spiritual strength.** Have there been times or seasons in your life when you've had a low or flippant view of the Lord's Supper? Why do you think that happened? How has this portion of the catechism shaped your understanding of the supper and countered faulty views?

4. **The depths of our discontent can only be satisfied by the abundance of the provision of Jesus Christ for empty sinners on the cross.** How does the Lord's Supper remind you of Christ's provision and your dependence on him? Reflect on how this practice helps you remember and rely on the sacrifice Jesus made for your sins.

5. **The Lord's supper is a foretaste of our joyous eternity with him.** How does the promise of future glory impact your participation in the Lord's Supper today? Reflect on how this forward-looking aspect of the supper provides hope and encouragement in your daily life.

SCRIPTURES TO PONDER

How do these Scriptures help us understand the meaning and significance of the Lord's Supper?

- **1 Corinthians 10:16-17:** "The cup of blessing that we bless, is it not a sharing in the blood of Christ? The bread that we break, is it not a sharing in the body of Christ? Because there is one bread, we who are many are one body, since all of us share the one bread."

- **Luke 22:19-20:** "He took bread, gave thanks, broke it, gave it to them, and said, 'This is my body, which is given for you. Do this in remembrance of me.' In the same way he also took the cup after supper and said, 'This cup is the new covenant in my blood, which is poured out for you.'"

- **John 6:53-56:** "Jesus said to them, 'Truly I tell you, unless you eat the flesh of the Son of Man and drink his blood, you do not have life in yourselves. The one who eats my flesh and drinks my blood has eternal life, and I will raise him up on the last day, because my flesh is true food and my blood is true drink. The one who eats my flesh and drinks my blood remains in me, and I in him.'"

PRAYER FROM CHURCH HISTORY

How good it is, Lord, to receive a broken Christ into a broken heart. We feed on your body broken, and your blood shed, as the sole, the only, the all-sufficient means of salvation by faith. Come then, dear Lord! Come to your own banquet, to your church, your table, your house of prayer, your ordinances! Come and bless your people! Amen.

—Robert Hawker (1753–1827)[1]

QUESTION 41
What Is the Bible?

ANSWER

The Bible is God's inspired Word that tells the story of the world and testifies to King Jesus. It is our supreme authority in faith and practice. God's Word is not a textbook we master but a world we inhabit, where we encounter the Divine Author who changes us.

SUMMARY

The Bible is God's inspired Word, telling the story of creation, fall, redemption, and restoration, with Jesus at its center. Far more than a religious text or collection of myths, the Bible is a living, Spirit-breathed narrative where God speaks to humanity. Through its diverse authors and genres, the Bible bears witness to Jesus and guides us in faith and life. It is not merely a book to be studied but a world to be inhabited, shaping our beliefs, values, and actions. As we read it, we encounter the Divine Author, who invites us into a transformative relationship with him.

REFLECTION QUESTIONS

Content in bold comes from *The Gospel Way Catechism*, pages 148-149.

1. **The Bible is the true story of the whole world.** When have you seen a personal or historical event reflect a truth found in the Bible? How does viewing your own life as a part of this narrative change how you see yourself? How does it run countercultural to today's focus on finding ways to earn cultural significance?

2. **Every story culminates in the life, teachings, death, burial, resurrection, and ascension of Jesus.** Is this a new idea for you? When did you come to see the big picture of Scripture? How has this been helpful in understanding how everything relates to Jesus?

3. **When we read the Bible, we are engaged in a practice that goes beyond the reading of mere words.** Do you personally encounter God when you read the Bible? When do you struggle to focus on reading the Bible?

4. **The Bible becomes the spectacles we look through to see and make sense of the world.** How has the Bible helped you understand and navigate challenging situations in your life? Reflect on how Scripture has provided clarity, guidance, or comfort during difficult times. How can you continue to rely on God's Word for direction?

5. **The Bible addresses sin and its consequences while offering hope and love.** How does the Bible's message of redemption and reconciliation influence your relationships with others? Consider how understanding God's forgiveness and grace impacts your interactions and how you can extend this love to those around you.

SCRIPTURES TO PONDER

What do these Scriptures teach us about God's revelation through his written Word?

- **2 Timothy 3:16-17:** "All Scripture is inspired by God and is profitable for teaching, for rebuking, for correcting, for training in righteousness, so that the man of God may be complete, equipped for every good work."

- **Psalm 19:7:** "The instruction of the LORD is perfect, reviving the soul; the testimony of the LORD is trustworthy, making the inexperienced wise."

- **Psalm 119:105:** "Your word is a lamp for my feet and a light on my path."

PRAYER FROM CHURCH HISTORY

Blessed Lord, who caused all holy Scriptures to be written for our learning: Grant us so to hear them, read, mark, learn, and inwardly digest them, that by patience and the comfort of your holy Word we may embrace and ever hold fast the blessed hope of everlasting life, which you have given us in our Savior Jesus Christ; who lives and reigns with you and the Holy Spirit, one God, forever and ever. Amen.

—THE BOOK OF COMMON PRAYER

QUESTION 42

What Is Prayer?

ANSWER

Prayer is communion with God in the name of the Son with the help of the Spirit. Prayer is a pursuit not of "mindfulness" but the mind of Jesus, through praise, confession, and petition. Its aim is not self-expression, but spiritual formation.

SUMMARY

Prayer is communion with God, a heartfelt conversation where we align our hearts and minds with his will. It goes beyond self-awareness, focusing on Christ-awareness and spiritual transformation. Through prayer, we experience God's presence, guidance, and grace, relying on the Holy Spirit to help us pray and shape our desires to match God's purposes.

REFLECTION QUESTIONS

Content in bold comes from *The Gospel Way Catechism*, pages 151-152.

1. **Prayer is a crucial way we become like Jesus.** How do you currently view the purpose of prayer in your life? Do you see it more as a means of self-expression or as a tool for spiritual formation? Reflect on how and why you usually pray and consider how you might shift your focus toward allowing the Spirit to shape and align your heart and mind with God's will. What changes could you make to deepen your practice of prayer as a way to become more like Jesus?

2. **The Holy Spirit is our guide in prayer.** Think about the many ways Western culture offers guides, influencers, and experts to help us in our life journey. How is the Holy Spirit uniquely better than the various gurus our culture offers?

3. **Christian prayer is not just about self-awareness but Christ-awareness.** It's surprisingly easy to think of prayer as a transactional exercise where we try to get things from God. This happens when we begin by thinking of ourselves and praying from there. The real goal of prayer isn't to get things from God but to grow in your relationship with God. Which way of prayer typically describes how you approach it?

4. **Prayer is an invitation to present yourself before God in all your mess.** How does this perspective change your approach to prayer? Consider how being honest and vulnerable in prayer impacts your relationship with God. How can you practice this kind of openness in your prayer life?

5. **Praise magnifies God's glory, confession deepens our intimacy, and petition reinforces our reliance on his wisdom and care.** Reflect on the importance of incorporating praise, confession, and petition in your prayers. How do these elements contribute to a balanced and meaningful prayer life?

SCRIPTURES TO PONDER

What do these Scriptures teach us about the meaning and significance of going to God in prayer?

- **Matthew 6:9-13:** "You should pray like this: Our Father in heaven, your name be honored as holy. Your kingdom come. Your will be done on earth as it is in heaven. Give us today our daily bread. And forgive us our debts, as we also have forgiven our debtors. And do not bring us into temptation, but deliver us from the evil one."

- **Philippians 4:6-7:** "Don't worry about anything, but in everything, through prayer and petition with thanksgiving, present your requests to God. And the peace of God, which surpasses all understanding, will guard your hearts and minds in Christ Jesus."

- **Romans 8:26:** "In the same way the Spirit also helps us in our weakness, because we do not know what to pray for as we should, but the Spirit himself intercedes for us with inexpressible groanings."

PRAYER FROM CHURCH HISTORY

Lord Jesus, give me a deeper repentance, a horror of sin, a dread of its approach. Help me to flee it and jealously to resolve that my heart shall be yours alone. Give me a deeper trust, that I may lose myself to find myself in you, the ground of my rest, the spring of my being. Give me a deeper knowledge of you as Savior, Master, Lord, and King. Give me deeper power in private prayer, more sweetness in your Word, more steadfast grip on its truth. Give me deeper holiness in speech, thought, action, and let me not seek moral virtue apart from you.

—Puritan Prayer[1]

What Is the Mission of the Church?

ANSWER

The mission of the church is to make disciples of King Jesus by declaring the gospel and displaying its power. The church is not a club, a charity, or a source of prosperity. In the power of the Spirit, we follow and obey King Jesus for the glory of God and the good of the world.

SUMMARY

The mission of the church is to make disciples of Jesus by proclaiming the gospel and living in its power. Unlike businesses or social organizations, the church is not defined by its structures or charity work. While the church may engage in acts of justice and compassion, its central mission is to call people to follow King Jesus in repentance and faith. Empowered by the Holy Spirit, the church exists for God's glory and the world's good, demonstrating the transformative power of the gospel in everyday life. The church is sent into the world to bear witness to Jesus and embody his kingdom.

REFLECTION QUESTIONS

Content in bold comes from *The Gospel Way Catechism*, pages 154-155.

1. **The mission of the church is to make disciples of King Jesus by declaring the gospel and displaying its power.** What are some common ways the church misunderstands mission? If this is not the main thing, then what are some typical ways other issues can become the main thing?

2. **The church lives according to the command of God to "act justly, to love faithfulness, and to walk humbly with your God" (Micah 6:8).** Does this describe the experience of mission in your own life and the life of your church? What needs to change in order to more faithfully align with this verse of Scripture?

3. **The abundant life promised by Jesus is not a life of wealth and possessions but a life of joy through self-giving love.** How does this perspective of abundance challenge the cultural emphasis

on personal prosperity? Reflect on how you can embrace and live out the joy of self-giving love in your daily life.

4. **We are transformed into salt and light (Matthew 5:13-16), so the world may taste and see that the Lord is good (Psalm 34:8).** How have you witnessed other Christians demonstrate the power of the gospel in their interactions with you and others?

5. **The church exists for the glory of God and the good of the world.** What does our culture commonly lift up as the ideals worth living for? Name a few of the ways in which it is countercultural to live for God and others in this self-centered culture we inhabit.

SCRIPTURES TO PONDER

What do these Scriptures teach us about the mission of God's people in the world?

- **Matthew 28:19-20:** "Go, therefore, and make disciples of all nations, baptizing them in the name of the Father and of the Son and of the Holy Spirit, teaching them to observe everything I have commanded you. And remember, I am with you always, to the end of the age."

- **Acts 1:8:** "You will receive power when the Holy Spirit has come on you, and you will be my witnesses in Jerusalem, in all Judea and Samaria, and to the ends of the earth."

- **2 Corinthians 5:20-21:** "We are ambassadors for Christ, since God is making his appeal through us. We plead on Christ's behalf: 'Be reconciled to God.' He made the one who did not know sin to be sin for us, so that in him we might become the righteousness of God."

PRAYER FROM CHURCH HISTORY

Lord, make me an instrument of Your peace. Where there is hatred, let me sow love; where there is injury, pardon; where there is doubt, faith; where there is despair, hope; where there is darkness, light; where there is sadness, joy. O, Divine Master, grant that I may not so much seek to be consoled as to console; to be understood as to understand; to be loved as to love; For it is in giving that we receive; it is in pardoning that we are pardoned; it is in dying that we are born again to eternal life.

—Francis of Assisi (1182–1226)[1]

Why Do We Tell People About Jesus?

ANSWER

We tell others about Jesus because of love: love for God who gave his only Son as the only Savior, love for our neighbors whose salvation we desire, and love for the gospel that reveals the truth about our world.

SUMMARY

We share the message of Jesus out of love—love for God, love for our neighbors, and love for the transformative power of the gospel. Unlike brand ambassadors who promote products for personal gain, Christians proclaim the gospel because it's the good news of salvation, not a commodity to be sold. Our love for God, who gave his Son as the only Savior, compels us to share this truth with the world. We desire for others to experience God's grace and eternal life. Evangelism flows from compassion, as we long for all people to turn to Jesus and be saved.

REFLECTION QUESTIONS

Content in bold comes from *The Gospel Way Catechism*, pages 157-158.

1. **We tell others about Jesus because of love: love for God who gave his only Son as the only Savior, love for our neighbors whose salvation we desire, and love for the gospel that reveals the truth about our world.** Reflect on your motivations for evangelism. Have there been times in your life when you were motivated by guilt or shame? Has someone ever made you feel like a bad Christian for not sharing the gospel with someone? How does this definition provide a better motivation?

2. **The gospel is not a product. Christians announce the gospel because the gospel is *news*.** Reflect on an experience where you shared the gospel with someone. How did the conversation unfold, and what insights did you gain from that interaction? Consider the impact the conversation had on both you and the person you were speaking with. What did this experience teach you about the importance of presenting the gospel as life-changing news?

3. **Evangelism flows from compassion, just as God's desire for people everywhere to turn from sin and turn to him in faith flows from his compassionate nature.** When was the last time you were

intentional about demonstrating God's love for others in your actions? How did it go? How have someone else's actions reflected God's love to you?

4. **We love the gospel because we've seen how powerful it is when the Spirit applies it to human hearts.** How has the gospel transformed your life, and how can you share this transformation with others? Reflect on your personal experience with the gospel's transformative power and how you can communicate this effectively to others.

5. **Our love for God, who gave his only Son as the only Savior, is the deepest motivation for our mission.** In the past, what has held you back from sharing the gospel? How can your relationship with God empower you to overcome this obstacle?

SCRIPTURES TO PONDER

What do these Scriptures teach us about our motivation and passion for telling others about Jesus?

- **John 3:16:** "God loved the world in this way: He gave his one and only Son, so that everyone who believes in him will not perish but have eternal life."

- **2 Peter 3:9:** "The Lord does not delay his promise, as some understand delay, but is patient with you, not wanting any to perish but all to come to repentance."

- **Romans 1:16:** "I am not ashamed of the gospel, because it is the power of God for salvation to everyone who believes, first to the Jew, and also to the Greek."

PRAYER FROM CHURCH HISTORY

Lord Jesus Christ, you stretched out your arms of love on the hard wood of the cross that everyone might come within the reach of your saving embrace: So clothe us in your Spirit that we, reaching forth our hands in love, may bring those who do not know you to the knowledge and love of you; for the honor of your name. Amen.

—*The Book of Common Prayer*

Why Do We Love and Serve Our Neighbors?

ANSWER

We love and serve our neighbors as a sign of the kingdom of God. We do good works not to prove our goodness or earn salvation, but as the overflow of God's love working in and through us.

SUMMARY

We love and serve our neighbors as a reflection of God's kingdom, not to prove our goodness or earn salvation. In a world where good works are often seen as a way to validate oneself or achieve righteousness, the Bible presents a different perspective. Our acts of kindness flow from God's love already working within us, not out of a need for self-validation. Empowered by the Holy Spirit, we can genuinely care for others without selfish motives. Our good works are a foretaste of God's kingdom, pointing to his justice and mercy, and offering a glimpse of what his reign looks like on earth.

REFLECTION QUESTIONS

Content in bold comes from *The Gospel Way Catechism*, pages 160-161.

1. **We love and serve our neighbors as a sign of the kingdom of God.** How does this perspective shape your understanding of good works? Reflect on how your actions toward others serve as a reflection of God's kingdom rather than attempts to secure your salvation. How does this viewpoint influence the way you approach opportunities to serve and care for others?

2. **Good works help us feel better about ourselves or prove our moral standing and worthiness.** Is there a time in your life when you would have agreed with this statement? What passages from Scripture refute this line of thought? How has your understanding of doing good works evolved over time? What experiences or teachings have helped you see good works not as a way to earn God's favor but as a response to his grace?

3. **Good works are more than displays of human kindness; they are demonstrations of God's love.** Our world thinks of acts of kindness as isolated gestures of goodwill. How does the Christian understanding of good works counter our culture's understanding?

4. **The presence of God's Spirit in us flows through us like a river, spilling over into kindness, compassion, and generosity toward others.** How have you experienced the Holy Spirit's empowerment in your acts of kindness and service? Reflect on specific instances when you felt guided and empowered by the Spirit in serving others.

5. **Our pursuit of justice is more than making the world a better place; it reflects the righteous character of God.** How can you align your efforts for justice and mercy with the gospel way? Consider how your actions can reflect God's character and bring about change in your community. How does understanding justice and mercy as expressions of God's righteousness shape your approach to social action?

SCRIPTURES TO PONDER

What do these Scriptures teach us about our good works in the world and our representation of King Jesus?

- **Ephesians 2:10:** "We are his workmanship, created in Christ Jesus for good works, which God prepared ahead of time for us to do."

- **Matthew 5:16:** "Let your light shine before others, so that they may see your good works and give glory to your Father in heaven."

- **Galatians 5:22-23:** "The fruit of the Spirit is love, joy, peace, patience, kindness, goodness, faithfulness, gentleness, and self-control. The law is not against such things."

PRAYER FROM CHURCH HISTORY

O Lord, reassure me with your enlivening Spirit; without you I can do nothing. Mortify in me all ambition, vanity, vainglory, worldliness, pride, selfishness, and resistance from God, and fill me with love, peace and all the fruit of the Spirit. O Lord, I know not what I am, but to you I flee for refuge. I would surrender myself to you, trusting your precious promises and against hope believing in hope.

—WILLIAM WILBERFORCE (1759–1833)[1]

QUESTION 46
What Is Worship?

ANSWER

Worship is the devotion we offer up to whatever we love most. Everyone worships. Christian worship is a lifelong outpouring of love to God, in humble adoration. Entranced by his beauty, we exalt him through praise and obedience.

SUMMARY

Worship is the outpouring of love and devotion to whatever we value most, whether it is God or idols. In our world, everyone worships something, placing ultimate worth on desires, goals, or even self. Christian worship, however, is directed solely toward God, acknowledging his supreme worth and holiness. It's not limited to religious acts but is a lifelong journey of adoration, praise, and obedience. As we worship, we reflect the beauty of the one we adore, growing in his likeness. Worship keeps us grounded, helping us resist idolatry and giving our lives purpose through devotion to God alone.

REFLECTION QUESTIONS

Content in bold comes from *The Gospel Way Catechism*, pages 163-164.

1. **Everyone worships.** Identify everyday objects or practices in our culture that people often elevate to a place of ultimate importance. What do these objects of worship reflect about the values of our society? How does the focus of our worship influence our lives and priorities?

2. **Christian worship is a lifelong outpouring of love to God.** When you examine your personal journey and relationship with God, what have been some ways you have worshiped God more in the last season of your life? When you look ahead to the next season of life, what are some areas in which you need to submit to and worship God?

3. **Our worship involves humble adoration.** How can you grow in humility? What views of yourself might you need to first let go of?

4. **We become what we worship.** How has your worship of God shaped your character and actions? Reflect on the ways worship has influenced your life and how you see the world. How can you continue to let your worship of God transform you into his likeness?

5. **Christian worship acknowledges God's supreme worth.** How does recognizing God's supreme worth impact your daily life and decisions? Think about how acknowledging God's worthiness changes your priorities and actions. How can you consistently honor God in your everyday life?

SCRIPTURES TO PONDER

What do these Scriptures teach us about the heart of worship?

- **Matthew 22:37-38:** "He said to him, 'Love the Lord your God with all your heart, with all your soul, and with all your mind. This is the greatest and most important command.'"

- **John 4:23-24:** "An hour is coming, and is now here, when the true worshipers will worship the Father in Spirit and in truth. Yes, the Father wants such people to worship him. God is spirit, and those who worship him must worship in Spirit and in truth."

- **Romans 12:1-2:** "Brothers and sisters, in view of the mercies of God, I urge you to present your bodies as a living sacrifice, holy and pleasing to God; this is your true worship. Do not be conformed to this age, but be transformed by the renewing of your mind, so that you may discern what is the good, pleasing, and perfect will of God."

PRAYER FROM CHURCH HISTORY

Merciful God, allow me to drink from the stream which flows from your fountain of life. May I taste the sweet beauty of its waters, which sprang from the very depths of your truth. O Lord, you are that fountain from which I desire with all my heart to drink. Give me, Lord Jesus, this water, that it may quench the burning spiritual thirst within my soul, and purify me from all sin. I know, King of Glory, that I am asking from you a great gift. But you give to your faithful people without counting the cost, and you promise even greater things in the future. Indeed, nothing is greater than yourself, and you have given yourself to mankind on the cross. Therefore, in praying for the waters of life, I am praying that you, the source of those waters, will give yourself to me. You are my light, my salvation, my food, my drink, my God.

—COLUMBANUS (540–615)[1]

PART 7

Future Hope

QUESTION 47
What Happens When We Die?

ANSWER

When we die, we do not cease to exist, neither do we become stars or angels. Our spirits soar to Christ, our hope in life and death, and our bodies rest until the resurrection.

SUMMARY

When we die, our spirits go to be with Christ while our bodies rest, awaiting resurrection. Contrary to common misconceptions, Christianity doesn't teach that we become stars or angels or exist forever as disembodied souls. Instead, we wait for the resurrection, when body and soul will be reunited, and we'll live with God on a renewed earth. Death is not the end, nor do we cease to exist. Jesus's resurrection promises life beyond death and ultimate restoration. Salvation is not an escape from creation, but its renewal, where God redeems both his people and the world from sin and death.

REFLECTION QUESTIONS

Content in bold comes from *The Gospel Way Catechism*, pages 168-169.

1. **Our spirits soar to Christ, our hope in life and death, and our bodies rest until the resurrection.** What are some popular cultural misconceptions about death and the afterlife? How does Christianity connect with the popular ideas and also counter them in a loving and hopeful way?

2. **Death does not lead to nonexistence.** How does the fact of life beyond death provide hope but also weight to your everyday life and interactions?

3. **Our spirits ascend to be with Jesus.** How does this belief help you navigate grief and find peace in the face of death? Consider how it influences your understanding of life, death, and the hope of eternal life with Christ.

4. **Salvation is not a rescue *from* creation; it's the rescue *of* creation.** How does this understanding of salvation influence your view of the physical world and your role within it? Consider how the belief in the restoration of creation affects your attitudes toward environmental stewardship in everyday life.

5. **The promise of being with Christ immediately after death.** How does this promise shape your perspective on the afterlife and the way you live your life now? Reflect on how the assurance of being with Christ influences your decisions, relationships, and priorities.

SCRIPTURES TO PONDER

What do these Scriptures teach us about our future with Christ?

- **1 Corinthians 15:20-23:** "As it is, Christ has been raised from the dead, the firstfruits of those who have fallen asleep. For since death came through a man, the resurrection of the dead also comes through a man. For just as in Adam all die, so also in Christ all will be made alive. But each in his own order: Christ, the firstfruits; afterward, at his coming, those who belong to Christ."

- **Philippians 3:20-21:** "Our citizenship is in heaven, and we eagerly wait for a Savior from there, the Lord Jesus Christ. He will transform the body of our humble condition into the likeness of his glorious body, by the power that enables him to subject everything to himself."

- **John 11:25-26:** "Jesus said to her, 'I am the resurrection and the life. The one who believes in me, even if he dies, will live. Everyone who lives and believes in me will never die. Do you believe this?'"

PRAYER FROM CHURCH HISTORY

Almighty God, it is the glorious hope of a blessed immortality beyond the grave, that supports your children through this vale of tears. Forever blessed be your name, for you have implanted this hope in my heart. If you have plucked my soul as a brand from the burning, it is not because you have seen any worth in me, but it is because of your distinguishing mercy, for mercy is your darling attribute. Clothe my soul with humility as with a garment. Let not a murmuring thought enter my heart, but may I cheerfully bear with all the trials of life. Clothe me with the pure robes of Christ's righteousness, that when he shall come in flaming fire to judge the world, I may appear before him with joy and not with grief. Amen.

—MARIA W. STEWART (1803–1879)[1]

QUESTION 48
What Happens to Those Who Oppose God?

ANSWER

God will one day purge the world of evil and establish righteousness on earth. Those who oppose God will experience eternal judgment—an everlasting fate apart from him, where his life and light are no more.

SUMMARY

Those who oppose God and persist in rebellion will face eternal judgment, separated from his life and light. While many today struggle with the idea of eternal consequences, the Bible teaches that God's justice requires the removal of evil to restore his good creation. Deep within, we all long for a world of justice and righteousness, but this means that evil must be purged, including those who reject God. Jesus's warnings about judgment serve as a loving call to repentance, urging us to turn from sin and find life in him, the only source of eternal hope and salvation.

REFLECTION QUESTIONS

Content in bold comes from *The Gospel Way Catechism*, pages 171-172.

1. **Those who oppose God will experience eternal judgment.** Does our culture believe in judgment and justice? What evidence supports that people do or don't? How is Christianity uniquely different to what our culture commonly believes about judgment?

2. **Turning our backs on God is what separates us from God's life and light.** Think of Adam and Eve turning their backs on God in the garden of Eden. How is every sin a similar act to that? How is repentance a literal turning to God?

3. **God must and will eradicate evil from the world and establish perfect righteousness.** Consider how recognizing our own sinfulness and the need for redemption shapes our view of God's judgment and deepens our appreciation for the profound mercy offered through Christ's sacrifice. Reflect on the relationship between God's justice and mercy, and how this understanding impacts

the way we live and interact with others. How does God's plan to eliminate evil from the world highlight his great mercy?

4. **Eternal judgment is the consequence of opposing God.** How do you reconcile the idea of a loving God with the reality of eternal judgment? Consider how the concepts of justice and love coexist in the biblical narrative and how this understanding affects your view of God's character.

5. **Now is the time to recognize the gravity of sin, turn from sin to Jesus in faith, and be safe with him.** How does the urgency of the final judgment influence your daily life and your approach to sharing the gospel with others? Reflect on how the reality of eternal judgment motivates you to live faithfully and witness to those who do not yet know Christ.

SCRIPTURES TO PONDER

What do we learn from these Scriptures about the fate of those who persist in unbelief?

- **Matthew 25:41-46:** "He will also say to those on the left, 'Depart from me, you who are cursed, into the eternal fire prepared for the devil and his angels! For I was hungry and you gave me nothing to eat; I was thirsty and you gave me nothing to drink; I was a stranger and you didn't take me in; I was naked and you didn't clothe me, sick and in prison and you didn't take care of me.' Then they too will answer, 'Lord, when did we see you hungry, or thirsty, or a stranger, or without clothes, or sick, or in prison, and not help you?' Then he will answer them, 'Truly I tell you, whatever you did not do for one of the least of these, you did not do for me.' And they will go away into eternal punishment, but the righteous into eternal life."

- **Revelation 20:11-15:** "I saw a great white throne and one seated on it. Earth and heaven fled from his presence, and no place was found for them. I also saw the dead, the great and the small, standing before the throne, and books were opened. Another book was opened, which is the book of life, and the dead were judged according to their works by what was written in the books. Then the sea gave up the dead that were in it, and Death and Hades gave up the dead that were in them; each one was judged according to their works. Death and Hades were thrown into the lake of fire. This is the second death, the lake of fire. And anyone whose name was not found written in the book of life was thrown into the lake of fire."

- **2 Peter 3:13:** "Based on his promise, we wait for new heavens and a new earth, where righteousness dwells."

PRAYER FROM CHURCH HISTORY

O holy God, righteous judge, my life terrifies me. A careful look discloses only sin and unfruitfulness, and what fruit that does appear is either so false, or imperfect, or in some way so corrupted, that it either cannot please you, or is absolutely displeasing to your eyes. How then can I possibly be saved? O Jesus Christ, for your name's sake, deal with me according to your name. Look on me with mercy, a miserable sinner, as I call upon you. It is true, O Lord, that my participation in sin calls for condemnation, and my penitence can never satisfy you. But it is also certain that your mercy exceeds all my offense. In you, O Lord, I put my trust. Amen.

—JOHANN GERHARD (1582–1637)[1]

What Is the Ultimate Hope for the Christian?

ANSWER

Our hope is Jesus Christ. We believe he will come again to reign over and restore the world, delighting to dwell with us and grant life everlasting, forever filling us with wonder, love, and praise.

SUMMARY

The ultimate hope for Christians is Jesus Christ, who will return to reign and restore the world. Our hope is not in human achievements or false promises but in the unwavering certainty of God's promises. Faith and hope unite in looking to Jesus, the fulfillment of God's Word, and his future reign. Christians believe that through Jesus's return, we will experience eternal life, joy, and peace in a restored creation. In the new heavens and earth, we will be free from sin, suffering, and sorrow, forever delighting in God's presence and living in eternal wonder, love, and praise.

REFLECTION QUESTIONS

Content in bold comes from *The Gospel Way Catechism*, pages 174-175.

1. **Our hope is Jesus Christ.** Reflect on how Christian hope is rooted in the certainty of God's promises and sovereignty, unlike general positive thinking, which lacks a solid foundation. Consider how this hope, anchored in Christ, provides a stable and enduring assurance that transcends circumstances, offering strength and peace in both trials and triumphs. How does this understanding of hope influence the way you approach challenges and uncertainties in life?

2. **He will come again to reign over and restore the world.** How is the promise of Jesus reigning and ruling a comfort to you? What are some specific things you can hope for within this promise?

3. **This hope fills us with wonder, love, and praise.** What are some common ways you are tempted to hope in and for things other than God? How is God a better hope than status, sex, or comfort?

4. **Delighting to dwell with us and grant life everlasting.** Reflect on the personal and communal aspects of Christian hope. How does knowing that Christ will return to dwell with us forever shape our current relationships and community life?

5. **Filled with wonder, love, and praise.** How can you cultivate a daily life that reflects the ultimate hope in Christ? Consider practical steps to keep your focus on the hope of Christ's return and how this can influence your actions, decisions, and worship.

SCRIPTURES TO PONDER

What do these Scriptures teach us about our ultimate hope through the resurrection of Jesus?

- **1 Peter 1:3:** "Blessed be the God and Father of our Lord Jesus Christ. Because of his great mercy he has given us new birth into a living hope through the resurrection of Jesus Christ from the dead."

- **Revelation 21:1-4:** "I saw a new heaven and a new earth; for the first heaven and the first earth had passed away, and the sea was no more. I also saw the holy city, the new Jerusalem, coming down out of heaven from God, prepared like a bride adorned for her husband. Then I heard a loud voice from the throne: Look, God's dwelling is with humanity, and he will live with them. They will be his peoples, and God himself will be with them and will be their God. He will wipe away every tear from their eyes. Death will be no more; grief, crying, and pain will be no more, because the previous things have passed away."

- **Titus 2:13:** "While we wait for the blessed hope, the appearing of the glory of our great God and Savior, Jesus Christ."

PRAYER FROM CHURCH HISTORY

You are God: we praise you;
You are the Lord; we acclaim you;
You are the eternal Father:
All creation worships you.
To you all angels, all the powers of heaven,
Cherubim and Seraphim, sing in endless praise:
Holy, holy, holy Lord, God of power and might,
heaven and earth are full of your glory.
The glorious company of apostles praise you.
The noble fellowship of prophets praise you.
The white-robed army of martyrs praise you.
Throughout the world the holy Church acclaims you;
Father, of majesty unbounded,
your true and only Son, worthy of all worship,
and the Holy Spirit, advocate and guide.
You, Christ, are the King of glory,
the eternal Son of the Father.
When you became man to set us free
you did not shun the Virgin's womb.
You overcame the sting of death
and opened the kingdom of heaven to all believers.
You are seated at God's right hand in glory.
We believe that you will come and be our judge.
Come then, Lord, and help your people,
bought with the price of your own blood,
and bring us with your saints
to glory everlasting.

—*Te Deum* (Ancient Christian Hymn)

QUESTION 50

What Does It Mean to Live in Light of the End?

ANSWER

We walk by faith, not in secular progress and technological advance,
but in the promise of God to reclaim this world and make everything
right. With hope, we await the return of the King we love.

SUMMARY

To live in light of the end means to walk by faith in God's promise to reclaim this world and make everything right, rather than placing hope in secular progress and technological advances. We focus on Jesus's return, allowing this hope to shape our lives, decisions, and priorities. By living with an eternal perspective, we engage in spiritual formation and obedience, countering the world's narratives of progress and fulfillment. Our hope in the return of our King provides strength and resilience, helping us endure life's challenges with a sense of purpose and anticipation.

REFLECTION QUESTIONS

Content in bold comes from *The Gospel Way Catechism*, pages 177-178.

1. **We walk by faith, not in secular progress and technological advance.** What are some common ways our cultural story leads us to focus on ever advancing and ever ascending in our progress? Reflect on the ways in which this is a wearying and burdensome way to live. Journal your reflections.

2. **The promise of God to reclaim this world and make everything right.** Reflect on areas in your life where your values, goals, and actions might be more focused on temporary or worldly concerns. What is needed to more fully lean into the promised future God is bringing? What do you need to start doing in your life to be ready for that? What do you need to stop doing as well?

3. **With hope, we await the return of the King we love.** Our world is full of anxiety. What would it look like for God's people to be a non-anxious kingdom presence in a world full of stress and inordinate desires? How is the assurance of Jesus's return a powerful engine for hope while we wait?

4. **Our world needs the hope we have.** How can you share the hope of Jesus's return with others in a way that is compelling and transformative? Consider practical ways to communicate the gospel message and the hope of Jesus's return to those around you.

5. **Living as citizens of heaven here and now.** How does viewing yourself as a citizen of heaven influence your interactions and relationships with others? Reflect on how this identity shapes your behavior, attitudes, and engagement with the world.

SCRIPTURES TO PONDER

What do these Scriptures tell us about living in light of the end?

- **Colossians 3:1-2:** "If you have been raised with Christ, seek the things above, where Christ is, seated at the right hand of God. Set your minds on things above, not on earthly things."

- **Hebrews 9:27-28:** "Just as it is appointed for people to die once—and after this, judgment—so also Christ, having been offered once to bear the sins of many, will appear a second time, not to bear sin, but to bring salvation to those who are waiting for him."

- **2 Peter 3:11-13:** "Since all these things are to be dissolved in this way, it is clear what sort of people you should be in holy conduct and godliness as you wait for the day of God and hasten its coming. Because of that day, the heavens will be dissolved with fire and the elements will melt with heat. But based on his promise, we wait for new heavens and a new earth, where righteousness dwells."

PRAYER FROM CHURCH HISTORY

Lord, nothing here lasts. *But I praise you that while all things perish, even the uttermost foundations of the earth, you are eternal, and if we cling to you and you embrace us with your love, then we will live forever in our true country, where finally our hearts may rest. I praise you for so great a comfort and salvation. Amen.*

—Tim Keller (1950–2023)[1]

Notes

Question 1: What Is the Center and Point of Everything?

1. Charles Taylor, *A Secular Age* (Belknap Press, 2018), 38.

2. Jonathan W. Arnold and Zachariah M. Carter, eds., *Cloud of Witnesses: A Treasury of Prayers and Petitions through the Ages* (Crossway, 2024), 32.

Question 2: How Do We see God and Come to Know Him?

1. Stanford Encyclopedia of Philosophy, "Protagoras," first published September 8, 2020, https://plato.stanford.edu/entries/protagoras/.

2. Adapted from *100 Prayers Every Christian Should Know: Build Your Faith with the Prayers that Shaped History* (Bethany House Publishers, 2021), 81.

Question 3: Who Does God Reveal Himself to Be?

1. All references to *The Book of Common Prayer* are adapted from the 2019 version (Anglican Liturgy Press).

Question 4: Who Is God the Father?

1. Robert Elmer, ed., *Grace from Heaven: Prayers of the Reformation* (Lexham, 2024), 242-243.

Question 5: Who Is God the Son?

1. Adapted from *100 Prayers Every Christian Should Know* (Bethany House, 2021), 21-22.

Question 6: Who Is God the Spirit?

1. Adapted from Tim Chester, *Into His Presence: Praying with the Puritans* (The Good Book Company, 2022), 42.

Question 7: Why Did God Create the World?

1. Carl Sagan, 1980s mini-series *Cosmos*.

2. Adapted from *The HarperCollins Book of Prayers*, compiled by Robert Van de Weyer (Castle Books, 1997), 148.

Question 8: What Is the Unseen World?

1. Adapted from *100 Prayers Every Christian Should Know* (Bethany House, 2021), 226-229.

Question 9: Why Did God Create Us?

1. Adapted from Dorothy M. Stewart, ed., *The Westminster Collection of Christian Prayers* (Westminster John Knox, 1999), 38.

Question 10: Who Are We?

1. Adapted from John Melvin Washington, ed., *Conversations with God: Two Centuries of Prayer by African Americans* (Amistad: Harper Perennial, 1995), 11.

Question 11: What Is Sexuality?

1. Ben White, "Ex-GI Becomes Blonde Beauty: Operations Transform Bronx Youth," *New York Daily News*, December 1, 1952.

2. Adapted from Robert Elmer, ed., *Piercing Heaven: Prayers of the Puritans* (Lexham, 2019), 152-153.

Question 12: What Is Our Responsibility?

1. Jonathan W. Arnold and Zachariah M. Carter, eds., *Cloud of Witnesses: A Treasury of Prayers and Petitions through the Ages* (Crossway, 2024), 7-8.

Question 13: What Is Work?

1. Adapted from Kurt Bjorklund, *Prayers for Today: A Yearlong Journey of Contemplative Prayer* (Moody, 2011), 222.

Question 14: What Is Rest?

1. Adapted from *The HarperCollins Book of Prayers,* compiled by Robert Van de Weyer (Castle Books, 1993), 175-176.

Question 15: What Is Freedom?

1. Robert Elmer, ed., *Grace from Heaven: Prayers of the Reformation* (Lexham, 2024), 59.

Question 17: What Form Does Our Sin Take Against God?

1. Adapted from *The HarperCollins Book of Prayers* compiled by Robert Van de Weyer (Castle Books, 1993), 58.

Question 18: What Form Does Our Sin Take Against One Another?

1. Adapted and abridged from Arthur Bennett, *The Valley of Vision: A Collection of Puritan Prayers and Devotions* (Banner of Truth Trust, 2002), 87.

Question 19: How Does God Respond to Sin?

1. Adapted from *ESV Prayer Bible*, Deuteronomy 26:1-15 (Crossway, 2019).

Question 20: Why Do We Feel Guilt and Shame?

1. Adapted from *The Complete Sermons of Martin Luther: Volume 5* (Delmarva Publications), 2000.

Question 21: What Is Suffering?

1. Adapted from Elisabeth Elliot, *Suffering Is Never for Nothing* (B&H, 2018), 54.

Question 22: How Does God's Rescue Plan Unfold?

1. Robert Elmer, ed., *Grace from Heaven: Prayers of the Reformation* (Lexham, 2024), 30.

Question 24: What Do We Learn from Israel's Kings?

1. *The HarperCollins Book of Prayers,* compiled by Robert Van de Weyer (Castle Books, 1993), 22.

Question 25: What Do We Learn from Israel's Prophets?

1. Jonathan W. Arnold and Zachariah M. Carter, eds., *Cloud of Witnesses: A Treasury of Prayers and Petitions through the Ages* (Crossway, 2024), 35.

Question 26: Who Is Jesus of Nazareth?

1. David Adam, *The Rhythm of Life: Celtic Daily Prayer* (SPCK, 1996), 48-49.

Question 28: What Happened on Easter?

1. Adapted and abridged from Arthur Bennett, *The Valley of Vision: A Collection of Puritan Prayers and Devotions* (Banner of Truth Trust, 2002), 48.

Question 29: What Does the Ascension Tell Us about Jesus?

1. Adapted from Thomas F. Torrance, *Christian Doctrine of God: One Being Three Persons* (A&C Black, 2001), 256.

Question 30: What Happened on the Day of Pentecost?

1. Adapted from Jonathan Gibson, *Be Thou My Vision: A Liturgy for Daily Worship* (Crossway, 2021), 61.

Question 31: What Is Repentance?

1. Adapted from Jonathan Gibson, *Be Thou My Vision: A Liturgy for Daily Worship* (Crossway, 2021), 115.

Question 32: What Is Faith?

1. To read the full Heidelberg Catechism, see "Heidelberg Catechism," Christian Reformed Church, accessed December 11, 2024, https://www.crcna.org/welcome/beliefs/confessions/heidelberg-catechism.

Question 33: What Is Union with Christ?

1. Jonathan W. Arnold and Zachariah M. Carter, eds., *Cloud of Witnesses: A Treasury of Prayers and Petitions through the Ages* (Crossway, 2024), 86-87.

Question 34: What Is Justification?

1. Adapted from Rick Brannan, *The Apostolic Fathers: A New Translation* (Lexham, 2017), 285-286.

Question 35: What Is Sanctification?

1. Adapted from *Phillis Wheatley: Complete Writings* (Penguin, 2001), 96.

Question 36: What Is Glorification?

1. Adapted from Robert Elmer, ed., *Grace from Heaven: Prayers of the Reformation* (Lexham, 2024), 74-75.

Question 37: What Is the Kingdom of God?

1. Adapted from *John and Charles Wesley: Selected Prayers, Hymns, Journal Notes, and Sermons* (Paulist Press, 1981), 59.

Question 38: What Is the Church?

1. From Jonathan W. Arnold and Zachariah M. Carter, eds., *Cloud of Witnesses: A Treasury of Prayers and Petitions through the Ages* (Crossway, 2024), 9.

Question 40: What Is the Lord's Supper?

1. Adapted from Robert Elmer, ed., *Piercing Heaven: Prayers of the Puritans* (Lexham, 2019), 144-145.

Question 42: What Is Prayer?

1. Adapted and abridged from Arthur Bennett, *The Valley of Vision: A Collection of Puritan Prayers and Devotions* (Banner of Truth Trust, 2002), 75.

Question 43: What Is the Mission of the Church?

1. Adapted from *The HarperCollins Book of Prayers,* compiled by Robert Van de Weyer (Castle Books, 1993), 150-151.

Question 45: Why Do We Love and Serve Our Neighbors?

1. Adapted from *100 Prayers Every Christian Should Know* (Bethany House Publishers, 2021), 33.

Question 46: What Is Worship?

1. Adapted from Thomas Oden and Joel Elowsky, eds., *On the Way to the Cross: 40 Days with the Church Fathers* (InterVarsity, 2011), 34.

Question 47: What Happens When We Die?

1. Adapted from John Melvin Washington, ed., *Conversations with God: Two Centuries of Prayer by African Americans* (Harper Perennial, 1995), 26.

Question 48: What Happens to Those Who Oppose God?

1. Adapted from Robert Elmer, ed., *Grace from Heaven: Prayers of the Reformation,* (Lexham, 2024), 114-115.

Question 50: What Does It Mean to Live in Light of the End?

1. Timothy and Kathy Keller, *The Songs of Jesus: A Year of Daily Devotions in the Psalms* (Viking Penguin, 2015), 252.

To learn more about Harvest House books and
to read sample chapters, visit our website:

www.HarvestHousePublishers.com

HARVEST HOUSE PUBLISHERS
EUGENE, OREGON